SORTIE

A BIBLIOGRAPHY OF
AMERICAN COMBAT AVIATION
UNIT HISTORIES
OF
WORLD WAR II

COMPILED BY

JOHN W. LAMBERT

PHALANX

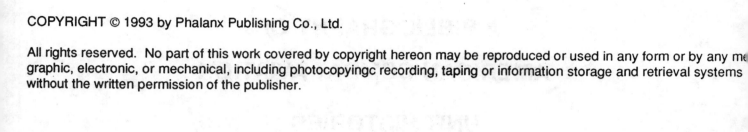

ISBN: 0-9625860-6-4

Compiled by John W. Lambert

Published by
Phalanx Publishing Co., Ltd.
1051 Marie Avenue
St. Paul, MN 55118 USA

Printed in the United States of America

TABLE OF CONTENTS

SORTIE

A BIBLIOGRAPHY

The passage of fifty years since the United States entered World War II has now properly conferred on that event the mantle of "history".

Five decades of healing and retrospection have finally permitted the veterans who served to reflect on their experience: the terrible losses of comrades, the months and years of combat. And in that same span, generations have grown up to contemplate, with awe, the reality of a nation determined and united against a common foe in a truly global struggle that ground on for over three and one half years and cost a million casualties. Studs Terkel called it, "the good war", a sobriquet that would never quite apply in subsequent military action.

Much of the history of World War II was recorded in the early post-war years in little noticed, limited edition unofficial unit histories. These journals, often just collections of photos, rosters and statistics, were viewed by academicians as little more than "class year books", memorials to small cliques of comrades in arms. Prized by the participants, they were tucked away on top shelves and in attics. As veterans bent to the task of rebuilding their lives and the nation, decades swept past and the old unit histories began to vanish, part of the flotsam of family living and moving.

Some of the statistics of World War II were lost between the combat zone and the archives but much was preserved to be incorporated into studious sets of service histories published in the post-war years. Regardless of the breadth of such multiple volume documentaries, students of history can do little more than grasp the broad strategy, the impersonal statistics of war, from these officially sanctioned accounts. However, some of the best data and much of the true experience of war is contained in organizational history volumes that describe war on the unit level.

In recent years both veteran airmen and a legion of post-war military/aviation history buffs have focused extraordinary national interest on the warbirds of World War II and the men who flew and serviced them. This bibliography is prepared in order to assist in the study of the great air war that ranged from Rabaul to Regensburg, an aerial conflict of such scope that it eclipses all those air wars before or since.

In the case of personal memoirs or recollections, the choice for inclusion was difficult. Some provide an excellent view of the unit in action, while others are narrowly personal, containing only scant connection or disjointed continuity with the definitive record of a unit. A few exhibit timeless prose, many are crude efforts. Except for those, "My Twenty-Five Year Career in the Air Force" type books, we have included all here so that the devotee of history may select from an array of battle experience, judging academic and literary merit for himself.

A more recent group of so called unit histories have been done through the collaboration of veteran's associations often with vanity publishers. These limited edition books are sometimes poor history, with an inordinate emphasis on unrelated anecdotes, before and after profiles of individuals and heavy emphasis on unit reunions. Nonetheless, all are included in this work.

How the Bibliography is Organized

This abstract focuses only on **combat aviation units**, with all due respect to the Ferry Squadrons, engineers, ground service units, etc. It is segmented first by service, then ascends from squadron level to higher command structures. In the case of the Navy we have chosen to include aircraft carrier histories when they also dealt with the resident air group

Authors in many cases are really editors, and in the immediate post-war era, histories were frequently the product of a team or a committee. Where names were available we have mentioned all. In some instances the name in the front of a history was merely the compiler, either a unit member or staff of the publisher or printer. From an abundance of caution all are shown in the "author" category.

The locale of the publication and the name of the publisher or printer is often unstated, hence their absence in this bibliography.

For easy reference we show the unit designation, therefore, we omitted a title where redundant: "The history of the so and so unit". Where meaningful titles or sub-titles were provided, they are so indicated.

It should also be noted that "pages" may refer to single sheets in a folio of loose documents, not always numbered pages.

INTRODUCTION (Cont.)

Thus the format for description of a work is as follows:
1. Author/editor/compiler (last name first),
2. **Title** (except as noted above),
3. Place of publication,
4. Name of publisher/printer,
5. Date of publication,
6. Number of pages,
7. Illustrations,
8. Color or art,
9. Soft or hard cover,
10. Information regarding successive printings.

Absence of any of these key elements merely reflects a lack of information or the failure of the document to disclose such matters.

For use in revised future editions of this volume, the publisher solicits data that will permit us to record missing works or flesh out bibliographies that are only partially covered herein.

Finally, for the benefit of used and rare book dealers, we have numbered each work - some 678 - and will also number subsequent additions that may be added to future editions.

GLOSSARY OF UNIT ABBREVIATIONS

AComdo	Air Commando	NFtr	Night Fighter
Bomb	Bombardment	Pat	Patrol
CAG	Carrier Air Group	PRecon	Photo Reconnaissance
ComCar	Combat Cargo	Pur	Pursuit
Comd	Command	Sq	Squadron
Comdo	Commando	TAC	Tactical Air Command
Comp	Composite	TC	Troop Carrier
Flt	Fleet	Trans	Transport
Ftr	Fighter	TRecon	Tactical Reconnaissance
Grp	Group	Wg	Wing
Lias	Liaison	WxRecon	Weather Reconnaissnce

AAF SQUADRONS

1st Ftr Sq	1	**The Fighting Furies**, 1945, 14 p.
2nd Ftr Sq	2	Burke, Lawrence G., and Curtis, Robert C., **The American Beagle Squadron**, Lexington, MA, 2nd Fighter Sq Assn., 1987, 499 p., illus.
2nd TC Sq	3	Smith, W.E., Cullman, Al, The Gregath Co., 1988, 430 p., illus.
4th Ftr Sq (Comdo)	4	1945, 39 p.
7th Ftr Sq	5	Gallagher, James P., **Meatballs and Deadbirds**, Perry Hall, MD, Jon Joy Publications, 1973, 121 p., illus.
8th PRecon Sq	6	Olsen, Harlan H., New York, NY, Ad Press, 1945, 217 p., illus.
9th Bomb Sq	7	Terry, Thurzal Q., **Strangers in Their Land**, Manhattan, KS, Sunflower University Press, 1991, 264 p., illus. Personal narrative.
9th Ftr Sq	8	Sydney, Aust., **The Flying Knights**, Angus & Robertson, 1944, 85 p., illus. A pictorial history.
9th Ftr Sq	9	Wandrey, Ralph H., **Fighter Pilot**, Mason City, IA, Stoyles Press, 1950, 82 p. Reprinted by Carlton Press, New York, NY, 1979.
10th ComCar Sq	10	Martin, John G., **Through Hell's Gate to Shanghai**, Athens, GA, Lawhead Press, 1983, 196 p., illus.
11th Bomb Sq	11	Cates, Michael D., Richmond, VA, Old Dominion, 1947, 104 p., illus.
12th TRecon Sq	12	1967, 78 p. History of unit in three wars.
12th TC Sq	13	**Memoirs**, 1944.
12th TC Sq	14	Donoven, John, 1945, 88 p. Largely cartoons.
13th TC Sq	15	Yoemans, William C., **Two Years c/o Postmaster**, Sydney, Aust., John Sands, 1946, 46 p., illus., some color.
14th Lias Sq	16	Dickinson, Charles S., Munich, Ger., R. Oldenbourg, 1945, 57 p., illus.
17th PRecon Sq	17	Hyland, Richard M., Martin, Charles T. and Vail, Richard M., **Strike**, Sydney, Aust., Jackson & O'Sullivan, 1945, 244 p., illus., crest in color, original art.
17th PRecon Sq	18	Olsen, Leonard and Shiffert, George A., Los Angeles, CA Brown & DeHaven, 1946, 127 p., illus.
19th Ftr Sq	19	Dallas, TX, Taylor Publishing Co., 1985, 128 p. illus. History of unit since 1917.
20th Photo Sq	20	1943, 30 p.
22nd Bomb Sq	21	Twees, Donald E., **The Bombing Bull Dogs**, Chicago, IL 1946, 52 p.
22nd Ftr Sq	22	Mahaney, Lloyd A, Gottingen, Ger., Muster-Schmidt, 1945, 88 p., illus., some color.

8

22nd Ftr Sq	23	Cupples, William H., **My Helpful Angel Flew With Me**, Harksville, NY, Exposition Press, 1975, 94 p. Personal narrative.
23rd TC Sq	24	1945, 20 p., illus.
25th Lias Sq	25	Leslie, P. Robert, Bradshaw Bros., 1984, 95 p. Personal narrative
26th PRecon Sq	26	Indiana, Aikin, 1945, 124 p., illus.
27th TC Sq	27	Burwell, Lewis C., Charlotte, NC, Lassiter Press, 1947, 130 p., illus.
29th TC Sq	28	Harkiewicz, Joseph, Orlando, FL 1990, 337 p., illus.
30th Bomb Sq	29	Sjostrom, Dorothea C., **Dick Smith, Bomber Pilot**, Beach Haven, NJ, 1944, 197 p. Personal narrative.
30th PRecon Sq	30	Gottingen, Ger., Muster-Schmidt, 1945, 48 p.
31st PRecon Sq	31	Flavin, John E. & Fletcher, William J., Nurnberg, Ger. 1945, 94 p., illus., cover colored.
32nd TC Sq	32	Van Reken, Donald L., Holland, 1989, 204 p. illus.
33rd PRecon Sq	33	Woodson, J.B., Jr., 1945, 46 p., illus. Pictorial history
34th Bomb Sq	34	Earl, O.K., **The Thunderbird Goes To War**, Springville, UT, Art City Publishing Co., 1947, 227 p., illus., cover in clor, hard bound.
34 Ftr Sq	35	1945, 60 p., illus
34th PRecon Sq *BILL ANDRES' SQ*	36	Hayes, William Donn, Jr. **Reflections,** 1981, 65 p., illus., original black & white drawings.
36th Bomb Sq	37	Carty, Pat, **Secret Squadrons of the Eighth**, Stillwater, MN, Specialty Press, 1990, 112 p, illus., art on dust jacket, hard bound.
39th Ftr Sq	38	Rothgeb, Wayne, **New Guinea Skies**, Ames, IA, Iowa State University Press, 1992, 200 p., illus., hardbound. Personal narrative.
39th Ftr Sq	39	Stanaway, John, **Cobra in the Clouds**, Temple City, CA, Historical Aviation Album, 1982, 48 p. illus.
41st TC Sq	40	Weinshelbaum, David B., **Downwind**, Philadelphia, Pa, Westbrook Publishing Co., 1950, 65 p., illus.
44th Ftr Sq	41	Starke, William H., **Vampire Squadron**, Anaheim, CA, Robinson Typographics, 1985, 207 p., illus., orig. art on dust jacket.
47th Bomb Sq	42	**The Crow Flight**, 1945, 87 p., illus.
47th TC Sq	43	Haffeman, Don, Skokie, IL, Intercollegiate Press, 1978, 565 p., illus.
50th TC Sq	44	DeMaria, Robert D., **The Unsung Heroes of World War II**,
54th Ftr Sq	45	Murray, Robert H., **The Only Way Home**, Waycross, GA, Brantley Printing Co., 1986, 159 p., illus.

54th TC Sq	46	San Angelo, TX, Newsfoto Publishing Co., 1946, 68 p., illus.
57th TC Sq	47	Healey, James M. and Pennock, H., **Saga of the Biscuit Bomber**, Sydney, Aust., Halstead Press, 1945, 131 p., illus.
60th TC Sq	48	Miley, Robert, **But Never a Soldier**, 1984
63rd Ftr Sq	49	Truluck, John H., **And So It Was,** Waterboro, SC, Press & Standard, Inc., 1988, 156 p., illus., soft bound. Revised edition 1989.
64th TC Sq	50	Sydney, Aust., Waite & Bull, 1945, 88 p., illus., some color.
65th Ftr Sq	51	**A Memoir of Michael Theodore Silver by His Parents**, 1947, 70 p.
66th Ftr Sq	52	**Call Jackpot**, Italy, 1945 49 p.
67th Bomb Sq	53	Lundy, Will, San Bernardino, CA, 1984, 355 p., illus.
67th Ftr Sq	54	Hq, Army Air Forces, **Pacific Counterblow,** Washington, DC, Govt. Printing Office, 1945, 56 p., ilus. Report on participation with 11th Bomb Grp, in battle for Guadalcanal.
67th TC Sq	55	Birdzell, Bill C., **Sky Train**, Sydney, Aust., Angus & Robertson, 1945, 234 p., illus., front cover colored.
68th Bomb Sq	56	Landy, **The Flying Eightballs**, Colorado Springs, CO Webb Todd, 1990, 445 p., illus, hard bound.
71st Ftr Sq	57	Arnold, Fredric, **Doorknob Five Two**, Los Angeles, CA, S.E. Maxwell, 1984, 274 p., illus., hard bound. Personal narrative.
72nd Lias Sq	58	Ably, Jean, Grenoble, Fr., B. Arthaud, 1946, 22 p., illus. Text in French. Author was Sq interpreter
74th Ftr Sq	59	Kissick, Luther C.Jr., **Guerrilla One**, Manhattan, KS Sunflower U. Press, 1983, 118 p., illus.
74th TC Sq	60	Boswell, Carl W., San Angelo, TX, Newsfoto Publishing Co., 1945, 47 p., illus.
75th Ftr Sq	61	Barnum, Burrall, **Dear Dad**, New York, NY, Richard R. Smith, 1944, 158 p. Personal narrative.
75th Ftr Sq	62	Little, Wallace H., **Tiger Sharks!**, Memphis, TN, Castle, 1987, 249 p., illus. Personal narrative.
79th TC Sq	63	Airgood, Roger,
81st Bomb Sq	64	**Back Roads to Freedom**, personal narrative.
81st TC Sq	65	Wolfe, Martin, **Green Light!** Philadelphia, PA, U. of Pennsylvania Press, 1989, 516 p., illus., hard bound.
83rd Bomb Sq	66	Newton Center, MA Modern Printing Co., 182 p.
84th TC Sq	67	Waltman, Charles, Mt. Prospect, IL, 1945, 125 p.
84th TC Sq	68	Guild, Frank H., Jr., **A Journey to the Far Shore,** Tyler, TX, City Printing Co., 1949, 142 p.

86th Bomb Sq	69	**The Lone Prowlers**, Washington, DC, Guthrie Litho Co.,
89th Bomb Sq	70	Houha, William F. & Stuntz, Conrad S., **Altitude Minimum**, Sydney, Aust., Angus and Robertson, 1945, 150 p., illus.
90th Bomb Sq	71	**Pair-o-dice, World War II Combat Log**, 1963, 469 p., illus.
94th Ftr Sq	72	Ilfrey, Jack and Reynolds, Max, **Happy Jack's Go-Buggy, Hicksville**, NY, Exposition Press, 1979, 167 p., illus., hard bound. Personal narrative of experience in 94th Sq and 20th Fighter Group.
94th Ftr Sq	73	Mullins, John D., **Hello Space Bar, This is Springcap**, Kerrville, TX, Hillside Cottage Publications, 1991, 172 p., illus. soft bound.
95th Ftr Sq	74	Carpenter, A.E., **We Are of Clay, Letters and Random Jottings of the Late Lt. "Chick" Rainear**, Philadelphia, PA, 1945, 95 p.illus., Houghton. Personal narrative.
96th Bomb Sq	75	Clausen, Walt, **GI Journey**, Seattle, WA, 1970, 101 p.
99th Ftr Sq	76	Halliburton, W.J., **The Fighting Red Tails**, New York, NY, 1978, 48 p.
99th Ftr Sq	77	Johnson, Hayden C., New York, NY, Vantage Press, 1987, 49 p.
107th TRecon Sq	78	28 p., illus., some color. History from WWI through WW II and post war service in ANG
109th TRecon Sq	79	1947, 34 p., illus.
109th TRecon Sq	80	Warren, Hoyt M., Abbevile, AL, Henry County Historical Soc., 1982 230 p. Personal narrative.
111th TRecon Sq	81	Densford, James T., **From Jennies to Jets**, 1973, 304 p., illus. some color. Fifty year history.
154th Wx Recon Sq	82	Gillies, Frederick W., Medford, MA, 1946, 137 p., illus.
160th TRecon Sq	83	Eschwege, Ger., 1945, 142 p., Illus.
319th Bomb Sq	84	Kenney, Roger B., **Aster Perious**, Sydney, Aust., Angus & Robertson, 1944, 62 p., illus.
320th Bomb Sq	85	Hodges, William C. and Sparks, William J. Jr., **Moby Dick**, San Francisco, CA, Schwabacher-Frey Co., 1945, 66 p., illus.
321st Bomb Sq	86	**Bombs Away**, Sydney, Aust., John Sands, 1944, 96 p., illus.
324th Bomb Sq	87	**25 Missions, The Story of the Memphis Belle**, New York NY, Training Aids Division, AAF, 1943, 36 p., illus.
341st Bomb Sq	88	Ijams, John H. Jr., 1948, 24 p. Personal narrative.
341st Ftr Sq	89	Borden, Horace L. Jr., 1947, 30 p. Personal narrative.
342nd Ftr Sq	90	Russo, Frank G., Jacksonville, FL, Douglas Printing Co., 1945,125 p.
342nd Ftr Sq	91	Wyper, William W., **Youngest Tigers in the Sky**, Palos Verdes, CA, 1980, 191 p., illus. Personal narrative.

345th Ftr Sq	92	McCann, Edward C., **Thunder Over Boxtown**, Pittsburgh, PA, 1949, 109 p., illus.
346th Ftr Sq	93	Grove, George B., Jenkins, Harold W., Kregloh, Edwin R., **The Memory is Still Fresh**, Houston, TX 1990, 300 p., illus., hard bound.
347th Ftr Sq	94	Schiffman, Charles, Stockton, CA, Atwood Printing Co., 1951, 159 p., illus. Hard bound.
350th Bomb Sq	95	Sheridan, Jack W., **They Never Had It So Good** , San Francisco, CA, Stark-Raith Printing Co., 1946, 165 p.
350th Ftr Sq	96	Bledsoe, Marvin, **WW II Fighter Pilot,** Oceanside, CA, 1980, 385 p. Personal narrative.
350th Ftr Sq	97	_____, Marvin, **Thunderbolt,** New York, NY, Van Norstrand Reinhold Company, 1982, 282 p., illus., hard bound. Personal narrative.
350th Ftr Sq	98	Price, Bill, **Close Calls**, Usk, WA, Aviation USK, 1992, 127 p., illus, soft cover. Personal narrative of two tour pilot.
356th Ftr Sq	99	Turner, Richard E., **Big Friend, Little Friend,** New York, NY, Doubleday & Co., 1969 176 p., illus., hard bound. Personal narrative.
369th Bomb Sq	100	**Combat Diary**, 1945, 142 p.
370th Ftr Sq	101	DeGrave, Ernest P., Pawtucket, RI, 1945, 80 p.
371st Bomb Sq	102	Moody, Dallas D., **Aerial Gunner from Virginia,** Richmond, VA, State Library, 1950, 366 p., illus. Personal narrative.
378th Ftr Sq	103	Kenaw, Charles F., Philadelphia, PA, Jeffries & Manz, 1946, 195 p., illus., cover in color.
400th Bomb Sq	104	Markham, Floyd A., **The Black Pirates**, Sydney, Aust., John Sands, 1945, 100 p., illus., cover in color.
404th Bomb Sq	105	Hora, Charles E., **We Were There**, Sacramento, CA, Pacific Litho. Co., 1946, 2 Vol.
405th Bomb Sq	106	**Green Dragons, Statistical Data,** 1945, 27 p.
406th Bomb Sq	107	See 36th Bomb Squad reference.
408th Ftr Sq	108	Sajed, Kemal, **Thunderbolt Odyssey**, Tulsa, OK, Stonewood Press, 1990, 160 p., illus., soft cover. Personal narrative.
409th Bomb Sq	109	Martin, Ralph G. **Boy from Nebraska, The Story of Ben Kuroki,** New York, NY, Harper Bros., 1946, 208 p., hard cover.
413th Ftr Sq	110	Birkett, Kenneth N., Bayshore, NY, Shelbrick Publishing Co., 1946, 36p., illus.
415th NFtr Sq	111	Sargent, Frederick O., Madison, WI, Campus Publishing Co., 1946, 79 p., illus.
422nd NFtr Sq	112	McEwen, Charles Jr., 1982, 111 p., ilus.

428th Ftr Sq	113	Steinko, John T., **Geyser Gang,** Minneapolis, MN, Roma Associates, 1986, 352 p., illus., hard bound.
430th Ftr Sq	114	Shennan, Alexander F., **The Backdoor Gang**, Ann Arbor, MI, Edwards Bros., 1950, 90 p., illus.
437th TC Sq	115	Guild, Frank Jr., **Action of the Tiger**, Tyler, TX, City Printing Co., 1950, 177 p., illus.
449th Ftr Sq	116	Harmon, Tom, **Pilots Also Pray,** New York, NY, Thomas Y. Crowell Co., 1944, 184 p. Personal narrative.
451st Bomb Sq	117	Lipkis, Leon G., Fresno, CA, 1947, 194 p.
464th Ftr Sq	118	**From Bruning, Nebraska to leShima,** 1946, 58 p., illus., original art, hard bound.
465th Ftr Sq	119	Saffern, Eugene L., **The Jug**, Ashland, OR, Ashland Printing Co., 1946, 72 p., illus.
484th Bomb Sq	120	MacIntyre, Becky, Papillion, 1984, 74 p., illus.
486th Ftr Sq	121	Sidney, Smiler, **Angus,** Norwich, Eng., Soman-Wherry Press, 1945, 46 p.
487th Bomb Sq	122	Trenton, NJ, Hibbert Printing Co., 1944, 181 p., illus.
487th Ftr Sq	123	**The Hunters,** 1945, 16 p., illus., cover in color.
488th Bomb Sq	124	Thomas, Everett B., **Round the World with the 488th**, Chicago, IL, Smith Printing, 1946, 178 p.
489th Bomb Sq	125	Caspar, Jack A. and Keljik, Ver, Minneapolis, MN Independent Press, 1947, 247 p., illus., hard bound.
491st Bomb Sq	126	Davenport, Douglas, **Achievements,** Calcutta, India, Baptist Mission Press, 1943, 72 p.
498th Bomb Sq	127	**The Falcons,** Oxford, MS, Mullen Printing Co., 1945, 84 p.
506th Bomb Sq	128	**The Green-Nosed Flying 8-Balls,** Dallas, TX, Taylor Publishing Co.1993, illus., hardbound.
508th Ftr Sq	129	**Dear Dick and App.,** 383 p.
510th Bomb Sq	130	1945, 242 p. *PART OF 351ST BOMB GROUP (B-17's)*
510th Ftr Sq	131	Mohale, Charles D., **Jenkins' Jerry Junkers**, CA, 1984, 140 p.
512th Ftr Sq	132	Brussels, Bel., Ad Goemaere, 1945, 26 p., illus.
513th Bomb Sq	133	Thomas, Rowan T., **Born In Battle**, Philadelphis, PA, John C. Winston Co., 1944, 367 p., illus. Reprinted by Zenger, Washington, DC, 1979.
514th Ftr Sq	134	Wegerski, Theodore E. and Mickwee, Sam, **The Raider Squadron**, Brussels, Bel., J.E. Goosens, 1945, 49 p., illus., some original art.

514th Ftr Sq	135	Beck, Levitt C., Jr., **Fighter Pilot**, Los Angeles, CA, Wetzel Publishing Co., 1946, 200 p.
525th Bomb Sq	136	Ellis, James F. and Linsky, William C.,**The Hun Busters**, Kimbolton, Eng., 1944, 42 p., illus., orig. cover art.
525th Ftr Sq	137	Blackwell, William H., Day, Harold R. and Duglay, Robert F., Heidelberg, Ger., Heidelberger, Gutenberg-Druckerei, 1945, 37 p., illus.
526th Ftr Sq	138	1945, 260 p., typed copy.
527th Ftr Sq	139	Howard, Sid, **Odyssey of an Invader Squadron, or Lost in Spaghetti Latitudes**, Italy, 1945, 20 p., typed copy.
530th Ftr Sq	140	Midwest City, OK, Scotch Directory and Mail Service, 1947, 76 p.
533rd Bomb Sq	141	Comer, John, **Combat Crew,** New York, NY, William Morrow & Co., 1988, hard bound. Reprinted by Pocket Books, 1989, 301 p., soft bound. Personal narrative.
557th Bomb Sq	142	Lundbert, Gust E. and Petersen, Karl S., 1945, 154 p.
723rd Bomb Sq	143	Cubbins, William R., **War of the Cotton Tails**, Chapel Hill, NC Algonquin Books, 1989, 267 p. Personal narrative.
756th Bomb Sq	144	Porter, Claude, **Cuckoo Over Vienna,** illus., hard bound. Personal narrative.
766th Bomb Sq	145	Barnes, William J.,Jr., **Toward Sanctuary,** 1945, 140 p.
775th Bomb Sq	146	Cassidy, Carl B., **Allyn's Irish Orphans**, Lime Srings, IA, Lime Springs Herald, 1946, 100 p., illus. Reprinted 1987
780th Bomb Sq	147	Davis, Charles, San Francisco, CA, 1946, 160 p.
781st Bomb Sq	148	Carl, Harry S., Dallas, TX, Taylor Publishing Co., 1989, 188 p., illus., hardbound.
783rd Bomb Sq	149	Gregory, Floyd E., Pantanella, Italy, 1945, 179 p.
820th Bomb Sq	150	1988, 37 p., illus.
868th Bomb Sq	151	Howell, Fred S., **The Snoopers**, New York, NY, Vantage Press, Inc., 1991, 147 p., hard copy.
873rd Bomb Sq	152	Kroesen, Paul, Buena Park, CA, West Orange County Publishing Co., 1946, 96 p., illus., some color.
873rd Bomb Sq	153	Herbert, Kevin, **Maximum Effort**, Manhattan, KS, Sunflower U. Press, 1983, 102 p., illus. Personal narrative.
885th Bomb Sq	154	MacCloskey, Monro, **Secret Air Missions,** New York, NY, R. Rosen Press, 1966, 150 p., illus.

AAF GROUPS

1st AComdo Grp	155	Claus, Dan G. and Schofield, Peter, **Light Planes**, Calcutta, Stateman Press, 1945, 98 p
1st AComdo Grp	156	Thomas, Lowell J., **Back to Mandalay**, New York, NY, Greystone Press, 1951, 320 p.
1st AComdo Grp	157	Sanders, Van Cortez, Jr., 1965, 47 p.
1st AComdo Grp	158	Prather, Russell E., **Easy Into Burma**, Dayton, OH, 1977, 91 p.
1st AComdo Grp	159	Van Wagner, Ralph D., Montgomery, AL, Air Command and Staff College, Maxwell AFB, 1986, 119 p., illus., soft cover.
1st AComdo Grp	160	**History of WWII Air Commandos**, Dallas, TX, Tayor Publishing Co., 1989, 140 p., illus. hardbound.
2nd Air Comdo Grp	161	See reference to **History of WWII Air Commandos**, Taylor Pub.
2nd Bomb Grp	162	Faig, Charles C., Italy, 1944, 34., illus.
3rd Air Comdo Grp	163	See reference to **History of WWII Air Commandos**, Taylor Pub.
3rd Bomb Grp	164	Larsen, Harald A., Martin, Charles P., Mandel, Edward, and Newmeyer, Frederick L., **The Reaper's Harvest**, Sydney, Aust., Halsted Press, 1945, 120 p., illus.
3rd Bomb Grp	165	Arbon, K. and Christensen, Chris, **The Bismark Sea Ran Red**, Marceline, MO, Walsworth Press, 1979, 314 p., illus, hard bound.
3rd Bomb Grp	166	Cortesi, Lawrence, **The Grim Reapers,** Temple City, CA, Historic Aviation Album, 1985, 105 p., illus., hard bound.
4th Ftr Grp	167	Gentile, Don S., **One Man Air Force as Told to Ira Wolfert**, New York, NY, L.B. Fischer Publishing Corp., 1944, 55 p., illus. Personal narrative.
4th Ftr Grp	168	Hall, Grover C., Jr., **Mr. Tettley's Tenants**, London, Eng., Baynard Press, 1944, 180 p.
4th Ftr Grp	169	Hall, Grover, **1,000 Destroyed**, Montgomery, AL, Brown Printing Co., 1946, 332 p., illus. Reprinted 1978 by Aero Publishers, Fallbrook, CA, and 1980 by Kensington Publishing with revision & update, hard bound.
4th Ftr Grp	170	Godfrey, John T., **The Look of Eagles**, New York, NY, Random House, 1958, 245 p. Personal narrative.
4th Ftr Grp	171	Fry, Garry L., **Debden Eagles,** New York, NY, Walker-Smith Inc., 1970, 102 p., illus., some color, soft bound.
4th Ftr Grp	172	Ethell, Jeffrey L. and Fry, Garry L., **Escort to Berlin,** New York, NY, Arco Publishing, Inc., 1980, 226 p., illus., some color, original art work on dust jacket, hard bound.

4th Ftr Grp	173	Dunn, William R., **Fighter Pilot, The First American Ace of World War II**, Lexington, KY, University Press of Kentucky, 1982, 234 p., illus, hard bound. Personal narrative of service with 4th and 406th Fighter Groups.
4th Ftr Grp	174	Goodson, James A., **Tumult In The Clouds**, New York, NY, St. Martin's Press, 1983, 283 p., illus., hard bound. Personal narrative.
4th Ftr Grp	175	Sagnulol, Mark M., **Don S. Gentile, Soldier of God and Country**, East Lansing, MI, College Press, 1986, 336 p., illus, hard bound. Biography of Gentile.
5th Bomb Grp	176	Mander, Alexander J., Raleigh, NC, Hillsborough House, 1946, 104 p., illus unit crests in color, hard bound.
5th Bomb Grp	177	Johnsen, Frederick A., **Bomber Barons**, Tacoma, WA, Bomber Books, 1982, 30 p., just illus., soft bound.
6th Bomb Grp	178	Rice, W.M., **Pirate's Log**, Manila, Phil., 29th Eng. Topo. Bn.,1946, 71 p., illus.
7th Bomb Grp	179	Shoup, Forrest, Carswell AFB, Ft. Worth, TX, 1948, 16 p., typewritten copy. Reprinted 1948.
7th Bomb Grp	180	Mitchell, John H., **On Wings We Conquer**, Springfield, MO, G.E.M. Publishers, 1992, 200 p., illus., hard bound. History of first year of WWII for 7th and 19th Bomb Grp.
7th PR Grp	181	USAAF, **Now It Can Be Told**, 7th Photo Group Assn., 1945, 62 p. Reprinted and revised in Phoenix, AZ, 1984, 245 p., illus.
8th PR Grp	182	USAAF, 653rd Eng. Bn., 1945, 32 p.
10th PR Grp	183	Ivie, Thomas G., **Aerial Reconnaissance**, Fallbrook, CA, Aero Publishers, Inc., 1981, 200 p., illus, soft bound.
11th Bomb Grp	184	See 67th Fighter Squadron reference, **Pacific Counterblow** .
11th Bomb Grp	185	Cleveland, William M., **Planes' Names**, Portsmouth, OH, 11th Bomb Group Assn., 1977, 100 p.
11th Bomb Grp	186	Cleveland, William M., **Grey Geese Calling**, Askov, MN, American Publishing Co., Inc., 1981, 492 p., illus, hard bound.
12th Bomb Grp	187	Wilson, Robert E., **The Earthquakers**, Tacoma, WA, Dammeier Printing Co., 1947, 150 p., illus.
12th Bomb Grp	188	Sexton, Winton K., **We Fought for Freedom**, Kansas City, MO, Burton Printing Co., 116 p.
14th Ftr Grp	189	Winooski, VT, 1945, 87 p. Reprinted in 1960.
15th Ftr Grp	190	Lambert, John W., **The Long Campaign**, Manhattan, KS, Sunflower U. Press, 1982, 186 p., illus, orig. art, hard bound.
16th Bomb Grp	191	USAAF, 947th Eng. Av. Topo. Co., 1945, 55 p.
17th Bomb Grp	192	Tannehill, Victor C., **Daddy Of Them All,** Arvada, CA, Boomerang, 1990, 80 p., illus., cover in color.

19th Bomb Grp	193	Taggart, William C. and Cross, Christopher, **My Fighting Congregation**, New York, NY, Doubleday, 1943, 176 p.
19th Bomb Grp	194	Ind, Allison, **Bataan: The Judgement Seat**, New York, NY, The MacMillan Comany, 1944, 395 p., hard bound. The Philippine air campaign with 19th Bomb Group and 24th Pursuit Group.
19th Bomb Grp	195	Crawford, William, Jr. **Gore and Glory**, Philaelphia, PA, David McKay Co., 1944, 192 p.
19th Bomb Grp	196	Union City, IN, 1947, 26 p., typed copy, illus.
19th Bomb Grp	197	Janin, Covington, **Mitsubishi Mission**, San Francisco, CA, Hooper Printing & Litho. Co., 1967, 34 p.
19th Bomb Grp	198	Parker, Van R., **Dear Folks**, Memphis, TN, Global Press, 1989, 289 p., hard bound. Personal narrative.
19th Bomb Grp	199	See 7th Bomb Group reference.
20th Ftr Grp	200	Steiner, Edward J., **King's Cliffe**, Long Island City, NY, 1947, 273 p., illus, hardbound. Reprinted 1989.
20th Ftr Grp	201	See 94th Fighter Squadron reference.
22nd Bomb Grp	202	Brosius, J.W., **The Marauder,** Sydney, Aust., Halstead Press, 1944, 120 p., illus.
22nd Bomb Grp	203	Schroeder, Frederick A., **Ducemus: We Lead,** 1985, 268 p., illus., original sketches, soft bound.
23rd Ftr Grp	204	Scott, Robert L., **God Is My Co-Pilot**, New York, NY, Charles Scribner's Sons, 1943, 277 p., illus., hard bound. Personal narrative.
23rd Ftr Grp	205	Cornelius, Wanda and Short, Thayne R., **Ding Hao**, Gretna, LA, Pelican Publishing Co., 1980, 502 p., illus.
24th Pur Grp	206	See 19th Bomb Group reference.
24th Pur Grp	207	Dyess, William E., **The Dyess Story**, New York, NY, G.P. Putnam's Sons, 1944, 182 p., illus. Personal narrative.
24th Pur Grp	208	Bartsch, William H., **Doomed at the Start**, College Station, TX, Texas A&M University Press, 1992, 504 p., illus. hard bound.
29th Bomb Grp	209	**Combat Diary**, San Francisco, CA, 1946, 28 p., illus.
31st Ftr Grp	210	Lamensdorf, Rolland G., Washington, DC, Kaufman Press, 1952, 79 p., illus.
31st Ftr Grp	211	Goebel, Robert J., **Mustang Ace**, Novato, CA, Prsidio Press, 1991, 304 p., illus. Personal narrative.
33rd Ftr Grp	212	**Combat Digest**, 1945, 24 p., illus.
33rd Ftr Grp	213	Reed, James E., **The Fighting 33rd Nomads**, Memphis, TN, Reed Publishing, 1988, Vol I, 354 p., illus., soft bound. Vol. II, 394 p., illus., soft bound.

34th Bomb Grp	214	Earl, Owen K., **The Thunderbird Goes to War**, Springville, MO, Art City, 1947, 227 p., illus.
34th Bomb Grp	215	Smith, Edwin S., Jr., San Angelo, TX, Newsfoto Publishing Co., 1947, 124 p., illus. Reprinted by Battery Press, Inc., Nashville, TN, 1981.
34th Bomb Grp	216	Hatch, Gardner and McAllister, Walt, Paducah, KY, Turner Publishing Co., 1988, 128 p., illus.
35th Ftr Grp	217	**Outcast Red,** personal narrative.
38th Bomb Grp	218	Henry, John, Manhattan, KS, Sunflower University Press, 1978, 48 p.
39th Bomb Grp	219	Palmer, Bernard, **Dangerous Mission,** Grand Rapids, MI, Zoneran Publishing House, 1945, 58 p.
40th Bomb Grp	220	Eustis, Lawrence B., San Angelo, TX, Newsfoto Publishing Co., 1946, 141 p., illus. Reprinted 1985.
40th Bomb Grp	221	McGregor, Carter, **The Kagu-Tsuchi Bomb Group,** Wichita Falls, KS, Nortex Press, 1981, 226 p., illus., hard bound.
40th Bomb Grp	222	Todd, Keith, Paducah, KY, Turner Publishing Co., 1989, 112 p., illus.
41st Bomb Grp	223	Ellison, Lee E., **The Forty First Service Record**, 1945, 45 p.
42nd Bomb Grp	224	**The Crusaders**, Baton Rouge, LA, Army & Navy Publishing Co., 1946, 204 p., illus.
42nd Bomb Grp	225	Smith, Paul T., **The Pacific Crusaders**, Reseda, CA, Mojave Books, 1980, 196 p., illus., hard bound. Personal narrative.
44th Bomb Grp	226	Harvell, Ursel P., **Liberators Over Europe,** San Angelo, TX, Newsfoto Publishing Co., 1946, 91 p. illus. Republished in 1982 by East Anglia Books.
44th Bomb Grp	227	Schuyler, Keith C., **Elusive Horizons,** New York, NY, A.S. Barnes, 1969, 176 p.
49th Ftr Grp	228	Kenney, George C., **Dick Bong: Ace of Aces**, New York, Duel, Sloan & Pearce, 1960, 166 p. Reprinted by Zenger Publishing Co., 1980.
49th Ftr Grp	229	McDowell, Ernest R., Carrollton, TX, Squadron/Signal Publications, Inc., 1989, 64 p., illus., some color, orig. art, aircraft profiles, soft cover.
51st Ftr Grp	230	Sullivan, John C., 1982, 99 p., illus. History from WW II through Korea.
52nd Ftr Grp	231	Suffolk County AFB, NY, 52nd Fighter Group, 1958, 40 p.
55th Ftr Grp	232	**Peter Eighty Comes To E.T.**, Wiesbaden, Ger., Paul Knoelber, 1946, 44 p.
56th Ftr Grp	233	Davis, Albert H., Coffin, Russel J., Woodward, Robert B., Washington, DC, Infantry Journal Press, 1948, 222 p, illus. Limited editions reprinted 1970 and 1987
56th Ftr Grp	234	Johnson, Robert and Caidin, Martin, **Thunderbolt**, New York, NY, Reinhart & Co., 1958, 305 p. Personal narrative of Johnson.

56th Ftr Grp	235	Mahurin, Walker, **Honest John**, New York, NY, G.P. Putnam's Sons, 1962, 313 p. Personal narrative of author in WW II and Korean wars.
56th Ftr Grp	236	Freeman, Roger, **Zemke's Wolf Pack**, New York, NY, Orion Books, 1989, 256 p., illus., hard bound. Zemke biography.
56th Ftr Grp	237	Hess, Wm N., **Zemke's Wolf Pack**, Osceola, WI, Motorbooks International, 1992, 128 p., illus, some color, soft cover.
56th Ftr Grp	238	Carrollton, TX, Squadron/Signal Publications, Inc., 1992, 64 p., illus., some color, orig. art, aircraft profiles, soft cover.
56th Ftr Grp	239	Gabreski, Francis, and Molesworth, Carl,**Gabby**, New York, NY, Orion Books, 1991, 227 p., illus, hard bound. Biography of WWII and Korean service of Gabreski.
57th Ftr Grp	240	Dodd, Wayne S., **The Fabulous Fifty-Seventh**, Marceline, MO, Walsworth Publishing Co., 1985, 181 p., illus., hard bound.
58th Ftr Grp	241	**Memoirs,** 1945, 250 p.
58th Ftr Grp	242	Kupferer, A.J. **No Glamour..No Glory**, Dallas, TX, Taylor Publishing Co., 1989, 320 p., illus., hard bound.
61st TC Grp	243	**Nomad's Story,** 1951, 48 p.
78th Ftr Grp	244	Hosford, Bowen I., **Duxford Diary,** Cambridge, Eng., W. Heffer & Sons, 1945, 151 p., illus., hard bound. Revised and reprinted 1975 by Roger A. Freeman and Michael J.F. Bowyer.
78th Ftr Grp	245	Fry, Garry L., **Eagles of Duxford**, St. Paul, MN, Phalanx Publishing Co., 1991, 144 p., illus., some color, original art color a/c profiles, hardbound.
79th Ftr Grp	246	Lind, Ragnar, **The Falcon**, Munich, Ger., F. Bruckmann, 1946, 286 p., illus.
79th Ftr Grp	247	Woerpel, Don, **A Hostile Sky**, Marshall, WI Andon Press, 1977, 260 p., illus., hard bound.
80th Ftr Grp	248	Breed, Warren, **Burma Banshee Combat Book**, Calcutta, India, 1945, 64 p.
82nd Ftr Grp	249	New York, NY, Robert W. Kelly Publishing Co., 1949, 115 p.
82nd Ftr Grp	250	Blake, Steve, and Stanaway, John, **Up and At 'Em!** Marceline, MO, Walsworth Publishing Co., 1992, 305 p., illus., some color, hard bound.
86th Ftr Grp	251	Los Angeles, CA, Montgomery Publishing Co., 1952, 107 p., illus.
86th Ftr Grp	252	Colgan, Bill, **World War II Fighter Bomber Pilot,** TAB books Inc., Blue Ridge Summit, PA, 1985, second printing Sunflowr U. Press, 1989, 210 p, illus., Personal narrative.
90th Bomb Grp	253	Segal, Jules F., **The Best Damn Bomber Unit in the World, The Jolly Rogers,** Sydney, Aust., John Sands, 1944, 112 p., illus.
90th Bomb Grp	254	Alcorn, John S., **The Jolly Rogers**, Temple City, CA, Historical Aviation Album, 1981, 212 p.

90th Bomb Grp	255	Lord, **Tales of the Jolly Rogers**, 1985, 337 p., illus.
91st Bomb Grp	256	**Statistical Summary**, 22 p., soft bound.
91st Bomb Grp	257	Stiles, Bert, **Serenade to the Big Bird**, London, Eng., 1947, 160 p. Reprinted by Bantam Books, New York, NY, 1984, 206 p. Personal narrative.
91st Bomb Grp	258	Moody, Samuel B. and Allan, Maury, **Reprieve From Hell**, New York, NY, Pageant Press, 1961, 213 p.
91st Bomb Grp	259	Brechler, **Wray's Ragged Irregulars**, 1945 interviews, published 1990 133 p., ring binder.
91st Bomb Grp	260	Duerkson, Menno, **Memphis Belle**, Memphis, TN, Castle Books, 1987, 334 p. Personal narrative.
91st Bomb Grp	261	Birdsong, G.P. Jr.,**Stormy Weather,** Pleasanton, CA, Hambleden Publications, 1988, 255 p., hard bound.
92nd Bomb Grp	262	Sloan, John S., **The Route As Briefed**, Cleveland, OH, Argus Press, 1946, 315 p., illus., hard bound. Reprinted by S. Wilson, St. Louis, MO 1976.
92nd Bomb Grp	263	Koger, Fred, **Countdown! 35 Daylight Missions Against Nazi Germany**, Chapel Hill NC, Algonquin Press, 1990, 183 p., illus. Personal narrative.
93rd Bomb Grp	264	San Angelo, TX, Newsfoto Publishing Co., 1946, 46 p., illus. Reprinted 1990.
94th Bomb Grp	265	Slater, Harry E., **Lingering Contrails of the Big Square** A, Murfreesboro, TN, 1980, 378 p., illus., hard bound.
95th Bomb Grp	266	Henderson, David B. and Dwyer, John P., **Contrails**, Cincinnati, OH, A.H. Pugh Printing Co., 1945, 250 p., illus.
95th Bomb Grp	267	Hawkins, Ian L., **Courage, Honor, Victory**, Bellevue, WA, 95th Bomb Group Assn., 1987, 357 p. illus.
95th Bomb Grp	268	Fletcher, Eugene, **Fletcher's Gang**, Seattle, WA, U. of Washington Press, 1988, 267 p. illus., hard bound. Personal narrative
95th Bomb Grp	269	Andrews, Paul, **Operational Record of the 95th**, 1989, 130 p.
95th Bomb Grp	270	Hawkins, Ian, **B-17s Over Berlin**, Washington, DC, Brassey's, 1990. 309 p., illus., art on dust jacket, hard bound.
96th Bomb Grp	271	Doherty, Robert E. and Ward, Geoffrey D., **Snetterton Falcons**, Dallas, TX, Taylor Publishing Co., 1989, 304 p., illus., hard bound.
97th Bomb Grp	272	**400 Missions**, Italy, USAAF, 1945, 8 p., illus. Statistical summary.
97th Bomb Grp	273	Owen, John H., Jr., Boston, MA, 1948, 24 p.
98th Bomb Grp	274	Baroni, George, **The Pyramiders**, Intercollegiate Press, 1978, 300 p., illus., hard bound.
98th Bomb Grp	275	Hill, Michael, **The Desert Rats,** Missoula, MT, Pictorial Histories Publishing Co. 1990, 120 p, illus., full color cover art. Just history of first Ploesti operation, Aug. 1943.

98th Bomb Grp	276	Hurst, David A., Paducah, KY, Turner Publishing Co., 1992, Vol. I, 240 p. illus. hardbound. Vol. II will contain post- WW II history.
100th Bomb Grp	277	Bennett, John M., **Letters From England,** San Antonio, TX, 1945, 132 p., illus. Personal narrative.
100th Bomb Grp	278	Nilsson, John R., **The Story of the Century,** Beverly Hills, CA, 1946, 222 p.
100th Bomb Grp	279	**100 Missions**, San Angelo, TX, Newsfoto Publishing Co., 1946, 222 p.
100th Bomb Grp	280	Callahan, John F., **Contrails**, New York, NY, John E. Callahan Associates, 1947, 284 p., illus.
100th Bomb Grp	281	Varian, Horace L., **The Bloody Hundredth**, Newton, MA, 1979, 174 p., illus.
100th Bomb Grp	282	Brown, James R., **Combat Record**, 1983.
100th Bomb Grp	283	Hawkins, Ian L. **Munster: The Way It Was**, Anaheim, CA, Robinson Typographics, 1984, 417 p., illus, hard bound.
100th Bomb Group	284	Brown, James R., and LeStrange, Richard, **Century Bombers**, Norfolk, Eng., 100th Bomb Group Memorial Museum, 1989, 242 p.
301st Bomb Grp	285	Muirhead, John, **Those Who Fall,** New York, NY, Random House, 1986, 258 p., sketches. Personal narrative.
301st Bomb Grp	286	Werrell, Kenneth P., **Who Fears**, San Antonio, TX, 301st Bomb Grp Ass'n., 1992, 300 p., illus., hardbound.
303rd Bomb Grp	287	Freeney, William A., **The First 300 Hell's Angels**, London, Eng., B.T. Batsford, 1944, 35 p., illus.
303rd Bomb Grp	288	Smith, Ben, Jr., **Chick's Crew**, Waycross, GA, 1978, 147 p., Personal narrative
303rd Bomb Grp	289	O'Neill, Brian D., **Half a Wing, Three Engines and a Prayer,** Blue Ridge, PA, Aero Publishers, 1989, 304 p. Personal narrative.
303rd Bomb Grp	290	Fleming, Samuel P., and Hall, Ed Y., **Flying with the Hell's Angels**, Spartenburg, SC, The Honoribus Press, 1992, 140 p., illus., soft cover, Personal narrative.
305th Bomb Grp	291	Morrison, Wilbur H., **The Incredible 305th: The "Can Do" Bombers of World War II**, New York, NY, Duell, Sloan, 1962, 181 p., illus. Reprinted by Berkley Publishing Group, New York, NY, 1984.
305th Bomb Grp	292	Thom, Walter W., **Brotherhood of Courage,** New York, NY, Martin Cook Associates, 1986, 246 p.
305th Bomb Grp	293	Craven, John V., **An Anthology**, Middletown, NY, 305th BG Assn, 1990, 349 p., illus., hard bound.
306th Bomb Grp	294	Bove, Arthur P., **First Over Germany,** San Angelo, TX, Newsfoto Publishing Co., 1946, 74 p., illus. Reprinted by Battery Press, Nashville, TN 1980 and enlarged to 138 p.

306th Bomb Grp	**295**	Strong, Russell A., **First Over Germany,** Winston-Salem, NC, Hunter Publishing Co., 1982, 334 p., illus.
307th Bomb Grp	**296**	Hamilton, Eugene K. and Harvey, Gordon, K., **We'll Say Goodbye,** Sydney, Aust., F.H. Johnston Publishing Co., 1945, 112 p., illus., orig. sketches, hard bound.
307th Bomb Grp	**297**	Boeman, John S., **Morotai: A Memoir of War,** New York, NY, Doubleday and Co., 1981, 278 p. Reprinted by Sunflower Univ. Press, Manhattan, KS, 1990, 283 p., illus., soft bound. Personal narrative.
307th Bomb Grp	**298**	Walker, Samuel I., **Up The Slot,** Oklahoma City, OK, Walker Publishing, 1984, 292 p.
308th Bomb Grp	**299**	Feuer, A.B., **General Chennault's Secret Weapon: The B-24 in China,** Westport, CT, Praeger Publishers, 1992, 264 p., illus., hard bound.
310th Bomb Grp	**300**	Hair, Charles A., **The Saga of '54 and More,** Anaheim, CA, Robinson Typographics, 1987, 210 p., illus., hard bound.
312th Bomb Grp	**301**	Sturzebecker, Russell L., **The Roarin' 20's,** Kennett Square, PA, KNA Press Inc., 1976, 301 p., illus., hard cover.
315th TC Grp	**302**	Brinson, William L., Rabat, Morocco, 1968, 49 p., illus. hard cover. Reprinted by Copple House Books, Lakemont, GA, 1984, 112 p.
316th TC Grp	**303**	San Angelo, TX, Newsfoto Publishing Co., 1946, 68 p., illus., hard cover.
318th Ftr Grp	**304**	**Highlights,** Ie Shima, 1945, 15 p., typed copy.
319th Bomb Grp	**305**	Corey, Wilfred G., **Bombs on the Target,** 948th Eng. Topo Co., Okinawa, 1945, 130 p., illus., reproduced from typewritten copy.
319th Bomb Grp	**306**	Oyster, Harold E.and Oyster, Esther M., **The 319th In Action,** Akron, OH, Burch Directory Co., 1976, 296 p., illus.
319th Bomb Grp	**307**	_____, Monroe, William B., et al, **Records,** 1976, 301 p.
319th Bomb Grp	**308**	Tannehill, Victor C., **The Big Tailed Birds,** Arvada, CA, Boomerang Publishers80 p., illus., full color soft cover.
320th Bomb Grp	**309**	_____, **Boomerang!,** Arvada, CA, Boomerang Publishers 1980, 307 p., illus, hard bound.
320th Bomb Grp	**310**	_____, **Saga of the 320th,** Arvada, CO, Boomerang Publishers, 1984, 78 p., soft cover.
321st Bomb Grp	**311**	Holloway, M.T., and McNevin, John L., Italy, 1945.
323rd Bomb Grp	**312**	Harlan, Ross E., 1945, 68 p., illus.
323rd Bomb Grp	**313**	Moench, **Maurader Men,** Malia Enterprises, Inc., 1989, 480 p., illus., hard bound.
323rd Bomb Grp	**314**	Moench, John O., **Marauder Men,** Longwood, FL, Malia Enterprises Inc., 1992, 480 p., illus., hard bound. Personal narrative.

324th Ftr Grp	315	Ziervogel, Frederick H., **The Odyssey of the 324th**, Paris, Fr., Printel, 1945, 52 p., illus., some color.
325th Ftr Grp	316	Hess, William N. and McDowell, Ernest R., **Checkertail Clan**, Fallbrok, CA, Aero Publishers, Inc., 1969, 98 p., illus., orig. art.
330th Bomb Grp	317	USAAF, 947th Engineer Avn. Topo. Co., 1946.
331st Bomb Grp	318	USAAF, 947th Engineer Avn. Topo. Co., 1945, 14 p.
332nd Ftr Grp	319	Francis, Charles E., **The Tuskegee Airmen**, Boston, MA,. Bruce Humphries, Inc. 1955, 255 p., illus., hard cover.
332nd Ftr Grp	320	Rose, Robert, **Lonely Eagles, The Story of America's Black Air Force in WWII,** Los Angeles, Ca, Tuskegee Airmen, Western Region, 1976, 160 p.
339th Ftr Grp	321	Harry, G.P. Paducah, KY, Turner Publishing Co., 1991, 257 p., illus. hard bound.
341st Bomb Grp	322	Claire, Thomas H., **Lookin' Eastward, A GI to Salaam to India,** New York, NY, 1945, 321 p.
342nd Bomb Grp	323	Moore, Carl H., **Flying the B-26 Marauder Over Europe,** Blue Ridge Summit, PA, TAB Books, 1980, 176 p.
345th Bomb Grp	324	Hanna, John C., Mortensen, M.H. and Witherell, William R., **Warpath,** San Angelo, TX, Newsfoto Publishing Co., 1946, 299 p., illus.
345th Bomb Grp	325	**Gunfight at Rabaul**, Birmingham, AL, Cather Publishing Co., 1974, 37 p. Story of the mission of Oct 18, 1943.
345th Bomb Grp	326	Blount, Ralph E., **We Band of Brothers**, Austin, TX, Eakin Publishing, Inc., 1984, 393 p., illus.
345th Bomb Grp	327	Hickey, Lawrence J., **Warpath Across The Pacific**, Boulder, Co., International Research and Publishing, 1984, 448 p., illus., some color, orig. art, hard cover. Reprinted.
347th Ftr Grp	328	Schiffman, Charles, Stockton, CA, 1947, 195 p., illus., hard cover.
347th Ftr Grp	329	Ferguson, Robert L., **Guadalcanal, The Island of Fire**, Blue Ridge Summit, PA, TAB Books, 1987, 256 p., illus. Soft cover
348th Ftr Grp	330	Wyper, W.W., **Youngest Tigers In The Sky,** CA, 1980, 191 p.
348th Ftr Grp	331	Stanaway, John, **Kearby's Thunderbolts**, St. Paul, MN, Phalanx Publishing Co., 1992, 112 p., illus., some color art, aircraft profiles, soft bound.
350th Ftr Grp	332	Milan, It., Pizzi e Pizio, 1945, 80 p., illus.
351st Bomb Grp	333	Harbour, Kenn, and Harris, Peter J., St. Petersburg, FL, Byron Kennedy and Co., 1980, 216 p.
351st Bomb Grp	334	Smith, Donald W., 1984. Personal narrative.
352nd Ftr Grp	335	Barlow, S.F., **Second To None**, 1945, 14 p., illus.

352nd Ftr Grp	336	Noah, Joseph W., **Wings God Gave My Soul, The Story of George E. Preddy, Jr.,** Alexandria, VA, Charles Baptie Studios, 1974, 209 p., illus. Reprinted by Motorbooks Int., Osceola, WI, 1991, 192 p., soft bound. Biography of Preddy
353rd Ftr Grp	337	Ivie, Tom and Powell, Robert H., **The Blue Nosed Bastards of Bodney,** Dallas, TX, Taylor Publishing Co., 1990, 292 p., illus., some full color, original art, hard bound.
353rd Ftr Grp	338	England, 1945, 8 p.
353rd Ftr Grp	339	Hess, William N. and Rust, Kenn C., **The Slybird Group,** Fallbrook, CA, Aero Publishers, Inc., 1968, 95 p., illus., orig. art.
354th Ftr Grp	340	**Close Calls**
354th Ftr Grp	341	Brown, Arthur F., **History In The Sky, 354th Pioneer Mustang Group,** San Angelo, TX, Newsfoto Publishing Co., 1946, 166 p., illus., some color.
354th Ftr Grp	342	Ong, William A., **Target Luftwaffe,** Kansas City, MO, Lowell Press, 1981, 335 p.
355th Ftr Grp	343	Marshall, Bill, **Angels, Bulldogs & Dragons,** Mesa, AZ, Champlin Fighter Museum Press, 1984, 178 p., illus.
356th Ftr Grp	344	Causer, H. Phillip, **"M.I.A.",** Norwell, MA, Phipps Publishing Co., 1977, 169 p. Personal narrative.
356th Ftr Grp	345	Miller, Kent D., **Escort,** Fort Wayne, IN, Academy Publishing, 1985, 185 p., illus.
357th Ftr Grp	346	Hayes, Robert W., **Escort,** England, 1945, 15 p. soft bound. Revised by James C. Aldrich and republished in Munich, Ger., by Thimayer, 1945, 24 p. soft bound.
357th Ftr Grp	347	Olmsted, Merle C., **The Yoxford Boys,** Fallbrook, CA, Aero Publishers, Inc., 1971, 103 p., illus., orig art.
357th Ftr Grp	348	Carson, Leonard K., **Pursue & Destroy,** Granada Hills, CA, Sentry Books, 1978, 175 p. Personal narrative.
357th Ftr Grp	349	Anderson, Clarence E. and Hamelin, Joseph P., **To Fly And Fight,** New York, NY, St. Martins Press, 1990, illus., hard bound. Personal narrative.
358th Ftr Grp	350	Ellison, Bruce G., **Orange Tails,** Chicago, IL, Rogers Printing Co., 1945, 216 p., illus,., some color.
359th Ftr Grp	351	Raines, Thomas H., Norwich, Eng., Soman-Wherry Press, 1945, 67 p., illus. Reprinted by Battery Press, Nashville, TN, 1978.
359th Ftr Grp	352	Miller, Kent D., **Jigger, Tinplate and Red Cross,** Ft. Wayne, IN, Academy Publishing Corp., 1987, 176 p.
362nd Ftr Grp	353	Gianneschie, Dan, **Morgan's Maulers,** Chicago, IL, Aires Press, 1981, 490 p., illus. Second edition printed 1986, 504 p.

363rd TRecon Grp	**354**	1945, 64 p.
363rd Ftr Grp	**355**	Miller, Kent D., **Seven Months Over Europe**, Hicksville, OH, 1989, 126 p., illus., soft bound.
364th Ftr Grp	**356**	**Operation Sunhat**, England, 1945, 16 p.
364th Ftr Grp	**357**	Joiner, O.W., Marceline, MO, Walsworth Publishing Co., 1991, 342 p., illus., hard bound.
365th Ftr Grp	**358**	Johnson, Charles R., **The History of the Hell Hawks**, Anaheim, CA, Southcoast Typesetting, 1975, 623 p., illus., hard cover.
367th Ftr Grp	**359**	Moody, Peter R., Manhattan, KS, Sunflower Univ. Press, 1979, 75 p.
367th Ftr Grp	**360**	Groh, Richard, **The Dynamite Gang**, Fallbrook, CA, Aero Publishers, Inc., 1983, 192 p., illus., original art on cover.
371st Ftr Grp	**361**	Baton Rouge, LA, Army & Navy Pictorial Publications, 1946, 198 p., some color, hard bound.
375th TC Grp	**362**	Finneran, John P. and Commell, Sam J., **History of the Tokyo Trolley,** Tokyo, Japan, Dai Nippon Printing Co., 1946, 31 p.
376th Bomb Grp	**363**	1945, 28 p.
376th Bomb Grp	**364**	McClendon, Dennis E., **The Lady Be Good: Mystery Bomber of World War II**, Fallbrook, CA, Aero Publishers, 1962, 205 p. Reprinted 1982. Story of the loss of one aircraft and crew.
376th Bomb Grp	**365**	Byers, Richard G., **Attack - Death In The Skies Over The Middle East,** Winona, MN, Apollo Books, 1984, 296 p.
379th Bomb Grp	**366**	Robb, Derwyn D., **Shades of Kimbolton**, San Angelo, TX, Newsfoto Publishing Co., 1946, 93 p, illus. Republished 1981
379th Bomb Grp	**367**	Bendiner, Elmer, **The Fall of Fortresses,** New York, NY, G.P. Putman's Sons, 258 p., illus, hard bound. Personal narrative.
379th Bomb Grp	**368**	Cassens, Kenneth H., **Screwball Express**, Paducah, KY, Turner Publishing Co., 1992, 160 p., illus., hardbound. History of a single aircrew.
380th Bomb Grp	**369**	Fain, James E., **The Flying Circus,** New York, NY, Commanday-Roth Co., 1946, 190 p., illus. Pictorial history.
380th Bomb Grp	**370**	Horton, Gary, and Horton, Glen, **King of the Heavies**, St. Paul, MN, 1983, 184 p., illus., some color, hard cover.
381st Bomb Grp	**371**	Westminster, Eng., Vacher and Sons, 1945.
381st Bomb Grp	**372**	Brown, James G., **The Mighty Men of the 381st: Heroes All**, Salt Lake City, UT, Publisher's Press 1986, 763 p., illus.
381st Bomb Grp	**373**	Comer, John, **Combat Crew**, Waco, TX, Texian Press, 1986, 268 p. Personal narrative.

384th Bomb Grp	374	Owens, Walter E., **As Briefed**, New York, NY, Edward Stern & Co., 1946, 210 p., illus. Addendum published 1974. Both volumes republished in Philadelphia, PA 1980.
384th Bomb Grp	375	Smith, Dale O., **Screaming Eagle: Memoirs of a B-17 Group Commander**, Chapel Hill, NC, Algonquin Books, 1990, 241 p., illus., hard bound. Personal narrative.
385th Bomb Grp	376	Leonard, Marston S., San Angelo, TX, Newsfoto Publishing Co., 1945, 58 p. Republished 1977.
386th Bomb Grp	377	Haire, T.B., St. Truiden, Bel. De Geneffe, 1945, 72 p., illus.
386th Bomb Grp	378	Young, Barnett B., **The Story of the Crusaders**, Ft. Myers, FL, 386th BG Assn., 1988, 192 p., illus., some color, original art, hard cover. Reprinted 1991.
388th Bomb Grp	379	San Angelo, TX, Newsfoto Publishing Co., 1946, 121 p., illus.
388th Bomb Grp	380	Huntzinger, Edward, San Angelo, TX, Newsfoto Publishing Co., 1973, 272 p., illus., hard bound. Revised and reprinted 1991.
389th Bomb Grp	381	San Angelo, TX, Newsfoto Publishing Co., 1946, 133 p., illus.
389th Bomb Grp	382	Ardery, Philip, **Bomber Pilot**, Hagerstown, MD, Univ. Press of KY, 1978, 233 p., illus. Personal narrative.
390th Bomb Grp	383	Milliken, Albert E., New York, NY, Eilert Print Co., 1947, 472 p., illus., some color.
390th Bomb Grp	384	Perry, Richard H., Richard, Wilbert H. and Robinson, William J., **The 390th Bomb Group Anthology**, Tucson, AZ, 390th Memorial Museum Foundation, Vol I, 1983, 306 p., illus., some color; Vol. II, 1985.
391st Bomb Grp	385	Walker, Hugh H., 1946, 132 p., illus. Reprinted by 391st Bomb Group Assn. 1990
392nd Bomb Grp	386	Vickers, Robert E., **The Liberators From Wendling**, Albuquerque, NM, 1972, 288 p. Reprinted at Manhattan, KS, by Sunflower U. Press, 1977.
394th Bomb Grp	387	Ziegler, Junior G. **Bridge Busters**, New York, NY, Ganis and Harris, 1949, 213 p., illus.
397th Bomb Grp	388	Beck, Henry C., Cleveland, OH, Crane Howard, 1946, 122 p., illus.
397th Bomb Grp	389	Stovall, James B., Jr., **Wings of Courage**, Memphis, TN, Global Press, 1991, 200 p., illus. Personal narrative.
397th Bomb Grp	390	Cassens, Kenneth H., **Screwball Express**, Paducah, KY, Turner Publishing Co., 1992, 160 p., illus., hardbound. Personal narrative.
398th Bomb Grp	391	San Angelo, TX, Newsfoto Publishing Co., 1946, 110 p., illus.
398th Bomb Grp	392	Ostrom, Allen, **Remembrances**, Seattle, WA, Vanguard Press, 1989, 100 p.
401st Bomb Grp	393	**200 Missions**, 1945, 12 p.

401st Bomb Grp	394	Closeway, Gordon R., San Angelo, TX, Newsfoto Publishing Co.,, 1947, 168 p., illus., some color, hard bound. A pictorial history.
401st Bomb Grp	395	Newcomb, Alan H., **Vacation With Pay**, Haverhill, MA, Destiny Publishing, 1947, 198 p. Personal narrative of POW.
401st Bomb Grp	396	Maher, William P. and Hall Ed Y., **Fated to Survive**, Spartanburg, SC, The Honoribus Press, 1992, 170., illus., soft cover. Personal narrative.
403rd TC Grp	397	**Two Years Pacific Sandman**, 1945, 27 p., typed copy.
404th Ftr Grp	398	Wilson, Andrew F., **Leap Off,** San Angelo, TX, Newsfoto Publishing Co., 1950, 230 p., illus.
404th Ftr Grp	399	See 408th Fighter Squadron reference.
405th Ftr Grp	400	Nolte, Reginald G., **Thunder Monsters Over Europe**, Manhattan, KS, Sunflower U. Press, 1986, 160 p. illus.
406th Ftr Grp	401	See 4th Fighter Group reference.
406th Ftr Grp	402	Beck, **Fighter Pilot**, Los Angeles, 1946, 200 p., illus. Personal narrative.
410th Bomb Grp	403	San Angelo, TX, Newsfoto Publishing Co., 1946, 80 p., illus.
410th Bomb Grp	404	Keim, Bill and Nan, **The 410th Book of Newsletters,** Autrain, MI, Avery Color Studio, 1987, 396 p., illus.
413th Ftr Grp	405	Tyler, Parker R., **From Seattle to Ie Shima**, Ie Shima, 1945, 30 p., typed copy.
417th Bomb Grp	406	Callanan, Lewis E., Green, Eugene L., and Keane, Paul A., **The Sky Lancer**, Sydney, Aust., John Sands, 1946, 113 p., ilus., crests in color.
433rd TC Grp	407	Holsoe, Torkel, **Back Load**, Sydney, Aust., Halstead Press, 1945, 248 p., illus., crests in color.
435th TC Grp	408	Gilmore, Lawrence J., and Lewis, Howard J., Greenville, SC, Keys Printing Co., 1946, 115 p., illus., crests in color, hard bound.
437th TC Grp	409	Guild, Frank H., Jr., **Action of the Tiger,** Tyler, TX, City Printing Co., 1950 177 p. Reprinted by Battery Press in Nashville, TN, 1980.
440th TC Grp	410	**DZ Europe**, Indianapolis, IN, Hollenbeck Press, 1946, 203 p., illus.
441st TC Grp	411	Frantz, Harry P. and Relvin, Joseph M., Taunton, Eng., E. Goodman & Sons, 1944, 48 p., illus.
442nd Bomb Grp	412	Paris, Fr., Curial-Archereau, 1945, 50 p., illus. in two volumes.
444th Bomb Grp	413	Harvel, Ursel P. **Liberators Over Europe**, San Angelo, TX, Newsfoto Publishing Co., 1945, 164 p., illus., crests in color. Reprinted 1982.
445th Bomb Grp	414	Birsic, Rudolph J., Glendale, CA, Griffin-Patterson Co., 1948, 81 p., illus. Supplement of 40 p. published 1950.

446th Bomb Grp	415	Castens, Edward H., San Angelo, TX, Newsfoto Publishing Co., 1946, 220 p., illus., crests in color.
446th Bomb Grp	416	Jansen, Harold E., The Hague, Neth., H.J. Zwennes, 1990, 319 p., illus., hard bound.
447th Bomb Grp	417	Dooley, Edward C. and Surridge, Estley K., San Angelo, TX, Newsfoto Publishing Co., 1946, 130 p., illus.
448th Bomb Grp	418	1975, 48 p.
448th Bomb Grp	419	Kramer, Ron V. and Michalczyk, Joseph T., and Hoseaman, James, **The 1000 Day Battle,** Lowestoft, Suffolk, Gillingham Publishing, 1979, 256 p., illus. Operations of the 2nd Air Div., particularly the 448th.
449th Bomb Grp	420	Turner, Damon and Lapham, Don, Collegiate Press, Vol. I, 1985, 360 p., illus, some color, hard bound. Vol. II, 1989, 466 p., illus, some color, hard bound.
449th Bomb Grp	421	**Tucson To Grottaglie,** San Diego, CA 1985, Vol. I, 360 p., Vol. II, 1990, 265 p. Hard bound.
450th Bomb Grp	422	**Cottontails,** Italy, 1945, 140 p.
450th Bomb Grp	423	Fagan, Vincent F., **Liberator Pilot: The Cottontails Battle for Oil,** Carlsbad, CA, California Aero Press, 1991, 145 p., illus., soft cover. Personal narrative.
451st Bomb Grp	424	Hill, S.D. and Hill, Michael, Paducah, KY, Turner Publishing Co., 1990, 240 p., illus., hardbound.
452nd Bomb Grp	425	Norwich, Eng., Jarrold & Sons, 1945, 22 p., illus.
452nd Bomb Grp	426	Barnes, Marvin E., Charlotte, SC, Delmar Printing, 1980, 280 p., illus., hard bound.
452nd Bomb Grp	427	Prewit, John, **The Lucky Bastard: Autobiography,** Bellevue, WA, 1983, 285 p. Illus., soft cover. Personal narrative.
453rd Bomb Grp	428	Low, Andy, **The Liberator Men of "Old Buc",** Rolla, MO, 1979, 178 p. Reprinted 1984.
453rd Bomb Grp	429	Benarcik, Michael, **In Search of Peace,** Wilmington, DE, 1992, 300 p., illus. some color, hard bound.
454th Bomb Grp	430	Barker, John S. Jr., **The Flight of the Liberators,** Rochester, NY, DuBois Press, 1946, 172 p., illus., crest in color. Reprinted by Battery Press, Nashville, TN, 1986.
456th Bomb Grp	431	456th Statistical Section, Italy, 1945, 72 p. illus.
457th Bomb Grp	432	Blakebrough, Ken, **The Fireball Outfit,** Fallbrook, CA, Aero Publishers Inc., 1968, 96 p., illus.
457th Bomb Grp	433	Byers, Roland, **Flak Dodgers,** Moscow, IN, Paw Paw Press, 1985, 272 p., illus., hard bound.

458th Bomb Grp	**434**	Reynolds, George A., Birmingham, AL. 1974, 64 p., illus. Second edition published 1979 and third edition enlarged in1988 by Taylor Pub. Co.
459th Bomb Grp	**435**	Italy, 1945, 28 p.
460th Bomb Grp	**436**	Devney, Edward J., Cleveland Heights, OH, 1946, 48 p., illus., hard bound. A pictorial history.
460th Bomb Grp	**437**	Newaby, Leroy W., **Target Ploesti - View From a Bombsight**, Novato, CA, Presidio Press, 1983, 272 p.
461st Bomb Grp	**438**	Italy, 1945, 48 p., illus.
461st Bomb Grp	**439**	**The Ringmasters**, Dallas, TX, Taylor Publishing Co., 1992, illus., hardbound.
462nd Bomb Grp	**440**	Oliver, Philip G., **Hellbird War Book**, Dallas, TX, 1946, 117 p., illus., hard bound.
462nd Bomb Grp	**441**	Morrison, Wilbur H., **Hellbirds**, New York, NY, Duell, Sloan and Pearce, 1960, 181 p., illus., hard bound. Reprinted by Zenger Publishing Co., Washington, DC, 1979.
463rd Bomb Grp	**442**	Rubin, Harold, St. Louis, MO, Becktold, 1946, 192 p., illus.
464th Bomb Grp	**443**	Callison, Talmadge P., **Hit the Silk**, New York, NY, Comet Press Books, 1954, 91 p. Personal narrative.
466th Bomb Grp	**444**	Woolnough, John H., **Attlebridge Diaries**, San Angelo, TX, Newsfoto Publishing, 1979, 218 p., illus.
467th Bomb Grp	**445**	Preston, Jack M. and Conway, Harris L., **Rackheath Memories**, Callahan, Eng. 1945.
467th Bomb Grp	**446**	Healy, Allan, Brattleboro, Eng., E.L. Hildreth & Co., 1947, 155 p., illus. Reprinted in North Tonawanda, NY, 1980.
468th Bomb Grp	**447**	Wolfe, Stephen, **The Story of the Billy Mitchell Group**, 1946, 135 p.
471st Bomb Grp	**448**	Loehr, Franklin D.., **We Don't Cry for Heroes**, Echelon Press, 1946, 124 p.
474th Ftr Grp	**449**	Calhoun, Jack and Beryl **Somewhere the Sun is Shining**, San Diego, CA, Grossmont Press, 1976, 70 p.
474th Ftr Grp	**450**	Keller, Isham G., **An Enlisted Man's Observations**, Minneapolis, MN, Roma, 1988, 128 p. Personal narrative.
475th Ftr Grp	**451**	**Satan's Angels**, Sydney, Aust., Angus and Robertson, 1946, 150 p., illus., some color.
475th Ftr Grp	**452**	Toll, Henry C., **Tropic Lightning**, Manhattan, KS, Sunflower U. Press, 1987, 136 p., composed entirely of line drawings by author accompanying letters home.
475th Ftr Grp	**453**	Brammeler, Charles L., Maxwell AFB, AL, Air University, 1987, 93 p.,Illus
475th Ftr Grp	**454**	Yoshino, Ronald W., **Lightning Strikes**, Manhattan, KS, Sunflower U. Press, 1988, 164 p., illus., orig art on cover.

479th Ftr Grp	455	Los Angeles, CA, Times-Mirror, 1945, 237 p., illus., hard bound.
483rd Bomb Grp	456	Epperson, William B. and Yudain, Bernie, Rome, It., Novissima, 1945, 158 p., illus., crests in color.
483rd Bomb Grp	457	Dye, John T., III, **Golden Leaves**, Los Angeles, CA, Ward Ritchie Press, 1962, 227 p.
486th Bomb Grp	458	**100 Missions**, Cambridge, Eng., Heffer and Sons, 1945, 28 p.
487th Bomb Grp	459	San Angelo, TX, Newsfoto Publishing Co., 1946, 109 p., illus., hard bound.
487th Bomb Grp	460	Lay, Bernie, Jr., **I've Had It**, New York, NY, Harper & Bros., 1945, 141 p., illus, hard bound. Personal narrative of Group CO. Reprinted by Dodd Mead, New York, NY, 1980.
489th Bomb Grp	461	Freudenthal, Charles H., Vienna, VA, 1989, 314 p, illus., unit markings and crests in color, hard bound.
490th Bomb Grp	462	Lighter, Lawrence S. and Holland, Frederick R., San Angelo, TX, Newsfoto Publishing Co., 1946.
491st Bomb Grp	463	Blue, Allan G., **Ringmasters**, 1964, 28 p., illus.
492nd Bomb Grp	464	_____., **The Fortunes of War**, Fallbrook, CA, Aero Publishers, Inc., 1967., 97 p., illus.
492nd Bomb Grp	465	Reynolds, George A., **European Theatre of Operations, Carpetbaggers**, Birmingham, AL, 1978, 23 p.
492nd Bomb Grp	466	Parnell, Ben, **Carpetbaggers: Ameriaca's Secret War in Europe**, Austin, TX, Eakin Publications, Inc., 1987, 204 p., illus., hard bound.
493rd Bomb Grp	467	San Angelo, TX, Newsfoto Publishing Co., 1946, 79 p., illus.
494th Bomb Grp	468	Williams, Jack J. and Woodward, Ernest L., **Kelly's Kobras**, Philadelphia, PA, W.T. Peck and Co., 1947, 147 p., crests in color.
497th Bomb Grp	469	Goforth, Pat E., **The Long Haul**, San Angelo, TX, Newsfoto Publishing Co., 1946, 54 p., illus., hard bound.
498th Bomb Grp	470	Ogden, Michael, 1945, 157 p., illus.
499th Bomb Grp	471	Burkett, Prentiss, Temple City, CA, **Historical Aviation Album**, 1981, 55 p., illus.
500th Bomb Grp	472	McClure, Glenn E., Riverside, CA, Rubidoux Printing Co., 1946, 100 p., illus., hard bound.
504th Bomb Grp	473	**Combat Diary**, 949th Eng. Avn. Topo. Co., 1946, 12 p., illus.
504th Bomb Grp	474	Midlam, Don S., **Flight of the Lucky Lady**, Portland Or, Binfords & Mort Publications, 1954, 208 p., illus. Personal narrative.
509th Comp Grp	475	Ossip, Jerome J., Chicago, IL, Rogers Printing Co., 1946, 56 p., illus.

509th Comp Grp	**476**	Marx, Joseph L., **Seven Hours to Zero**, New York, NY, G.P. Putnam's Sons, 1967, 256 p.
509th Comp Grp	**477**	Thomas Gordon, and Witts, Max M., **Ruin From the Air**, London, Eng., Hamilton, 1977, 386 p.
509th Comp Grp	**478**	Tibbets, Paul W., **Flight of the Enola Gay**, Reynoldsburg, OH, Buckeye Aviation Book Co., 1989, 316 p. Personal narrtive of a/c commander of first A-bomb mission.

SEE PGS 266 IN BOOK   CORTESI, LAWRENCE, OPERATION CARTWHEEL

AAF WINGS

1st Bomb Wg	479	Bishop, Cliff T., **Fortresses of the Big Triangle First,** Bishops Stortford, East Anglia, Eng., 1986, 320 p., illus., hard bound. A pictorial and statistical record of several VIII AF groups.
14th Bomb Wg	480	Taylor, William B., San Angelo, TX, Newsfoto Publishing Co., 1945, 66 p., illus.
14th Bomb Wg	481	North, Tony, and Bailey, Mike, **Liberator Album, Vol II**, 1981,
20th Bomb Wg	482	_____, **Liberator Album, Vol I,** 1979
47th Bomb Wg	483	Cerra, Frank R. and Stoolman, Herbert L., Sioux City, IA, Perkins Brothers Co., 1946, 94 p., illus.
50th TC Wg	484	**Invaders**, Paris, Fr., Desfosses-Neogravure, 1945, 36 p, illus.
53rd TC Wg	485	**Ever First**, Paris, Fr., Desfosses-Neogravure, 1945, 36 p., illus.
54th TC Wg	486	Jacobson, Richard S., **Morseby to Manila**, Sydney, Aust., Angus & Robertson, 1945, 278 p., illus.
57th Bomb Wg	487	941st Eng. Bn., 1945, 109 p., illus., reproduced from typed copy.
64th Ftr Wg	488	Campbell, Harlan S., Cambell, Philip S. and Lexcen, John M., Tubingen, Ger., Laupp, 1945, 199 p., illus.
66th Ftr Wg	489	Carpenter, Newt and Houston, Karl H., **One Story, Two Worlds, Three Enemies, Four Freedoms**, Cambridge, Eng., W. Heffer & Sons, 1945, 24 p., illus.
73rd Bomb Wg	490	San Angelo, TX, Newsfoto, 1946, 202 p., illus. Reprinted Nashville, TN, The Battery Press, 1989,
93rd Bomb Wg	491	**100 Missions**, San Angelo, TX, Newsfoto Publishing Co., 1946, 38 p., illus., hard bound.
96th Bomb Wg	492	North, Tony, and Bailey, Mike, **Liberator Album, Vol III,** 1984
308th Bomb Wg	493	Herring, Robert R., **From Dobdura to Okinawa**, San Angelo, TX, Newsfoto Publishing Co., 1946, 98 p., illus.
314th Bomb Wg	494	Laird, Robert E., **Maximum Effort**, Rutland, VT, Academy Books, 1989, 226 p., illus., hard bound. Reprinted 1990.
315th Bomb Wg	495	Harrington, George E., and Leasure, William, St. Petersburg, FL, Kennedy, 1985, 256 p., illus., hard bound.
392nd Trans Wg	496	901st AF HQ Co., 52 p., illus.
Chinese-American Composite Wing	497	Kebric, Harry L., **Dragon Tigers**, New York, NY, Vantage Press, 1971, 137 p., illus. Personal narrative of Intelligence Officer.
Chinese American Composite Wing	498	Molesworth, Carl, **Wing to Wing**, Orion Books, 1990, 230 p., illus., hard bound.

China-India Wg ATC **499** Tunner, Wm H., **Over the Hump**, New York, NY, Duell, Sloan, 1964, 335 p., illus., hard bound. Autobiography of CO.

China-India Wg ATC **500** Thorne, Bliss K., **The Hump: The Great Himalayan Airlift of WWII**, Philadelphia, PA, Lippincott, 1965, 185 p., illus., hardbound.

China-India Wg ATC **501** White, Edwin L., **Ten Thousand Tons by Christmas**, St. Petersburg, FL, Valkyrie Press, 1977, 255 p., illus., hardbound.

China-India Wg ATC **502** **History of the Hump Pilots**, Dallas, TX, Taylor Publishing Co., 1980, 596 p., Vol. I and II, hardbound.

China-India Wg ATC **503** Brewer, James F., **China Airlift - The Hump**, Paducah, KY, Turner Publishing Co., 1980, Vol. I, 600 p., illus., some color, hard bound.

China-India Wg ATC **504** Howton, Harry G., **China Airlift - The Hump**, Paducah, KY, Turner Publishing Co., 1983, Vol II, 628 p., illus., some color, hard bound.

China-India Wg ATC **505** Spencer, Otha C. **Flying the Hump**, College Station, TX, Texas A&M University Press, 1992, 240 p., illus., hardbound

China-India Wg ATC **506** Theis, Janes and Martin, John G., **China Airlift - The Hump,** Paducah, KY, Turner Publishing Co., 1992, Vol. III, 372 p., some color, hard bound.

AAF NUMBERED COMMANDS

5th AF	507	Hq, AAF, New York, 1945, 6 p. Reproduced from typed copy.
5th AF	508	U.S. Strategic Bombing Survey, Military analysis Division, **The Fifth Air Force Against Japan**, Washington, DC, Govt. Printing Office, 1947, 114 p.
5th AF	509	Bozung, Jack H., **The 5th Over the Southwest Pacific**, Los Angeles, Ca, AAF Publications Co., 1947, 40 p., illus.
5th AF	510	**Rabaul, 2 November 1943,** Washington, DC, Govt. Printing Office, 1944, 12 p., illus., spiral binder.
5th AF	511	Sinton, Russel L. and Schloss, Leon, **The Menace From Moresby**, San Angelo, TX, Newsfoto Publishing Co., 1950, 109 p., illus. Republished by Battery Press, Nashville, TN and enlarged to 216 p., hard bound.
5th Ftr Comd	512	Wistranad, R.B., **Pacific Sweep**, Sydney, Aust., F.H. Johnston Publishing Co., 1945, 112 p., illus.
5th AF	513	Rust, Kenn C., Temple City, CA, Historic Aviation Album, 1973, 64 p., illus., line drawings, color on soft cover. Reprinted by Sunshine House, Terre Haute, IN, 1992.
5th AF	514	Birdsall, Steve, **Flying Buccaneers**, Garden City, NY, Doubleday & Co., Inc., 1977, 312 p., illus., line drawings in color., hard bound.
5 & 13 Ftr Comd	515	Hess, William N., **Pacific Sweep,** Garden City, NY, Doubleday & Company, Inc., 1974, 278 p., illus., hard bound.
7th AF	516	Public Relations Office, Seventh Air Force, 955th Eng. Topo. Co., 1945, 12 p., illus., soft cover.
7th AF	517	Howard, Clive and Whitley, Joe, **One Damned Island After Another**, Chapel Hill, NC, Univ. of NC Press, 1946, 403 p., illus., hard bound. Reprinted by Zenger Publishing Co., 1978.
7th AF	518	Fern, Stewart, **Wings Over the Pacific**, Fostoria, OH, The Gray Printing Co., 1947, 118 p., illus., hard bound a pictorial history.
7th AF	519	Rust, Kenn C., Temple City, CA, Historical Aviation Album1978, 64 p., line drawings, color on soft cover. Reprinted by Sunshine Huse, Terre Haute, IN, 1992
7th Ftr Comd	520	Lambert, John W., **The Pineapple Air Force: Pearl Harbor to Tokyo**, St. Paul, MN, Phalanx Publishing Co., 1990, 220 p., illus., some color,aircraft profiles, hard bound.
8th AF	521	Hq, AAF, **Sunday Punch in Normandy**, Washington, DC, Govt. Printing Office, 1945, 32 p., illus., soft cover in color.
8th AF	522	Bozung, Jack H., **The Eighth Sees England**, Los Angeles, Ca, AAF Publilcation Co., 1946, 40 p., illus.

8th AF	523	Peaslee, Budd J., **Heritage of Valor**, Philadelphia, PA, J.D. Lippincott Company, 1964, 288 p., illus., hard bound. Personal narrative.
8TH AF	—	ASTOR, GERALD, THE MIGHTY EIGHTH. DELL PUBLISHING 1987
8th AF	524	Freeman, Roger A., **The Mighty Eighth,** New York, NY, Doubleday & Co., Inc., 1970, 311 p., illus., hard bound.
8th AF	525	Rust, Kenn C., **Eighth Air Force Story**, Temple City, CA, Historical Aviation Album, 1978, 73 p., illus., color on cover, soft bound. Reprinted by Sunshine House, Terre Haute, IN, 1992
8th AF	526	Woolnough, John H., **The 8th Air Force Album:**. San Angelo, TX, Newsfoto Publishing, 1981, 224 p., illus.
8th AF	527	Freeman, Roger A., **The Mighty Eighth War Diary**, Osceola, WI, Motorbooks International., 1990, 512 p., illus., hard bound.
8th Bomb Comd	528	USAF, **Target: Germany, First Year Over Europe**, New York, NY, Simon & Schuster, 1943, 121 p., illus., soft bound.
8th Ftr Comd	529	Farnol, Lynn, **To The Limit of Their Endurance**, Manhattan, KS, Sunflower University Press, 1986, 100 p., soft bound.
8th Ftr Comd	530	Scutts, Jerry, **Lion In The Sky**, London, P. Stephens, 1987, 152 p., illus., hard bound.
8th Ftr Comd	531	Hess, William N. and Ivie, Thomas G., Osciola, WI, Motorbooks International, 1990, 264 p., illus., some color, d.j. full color, hardbound.
8th Ftr Comd	532	Ethell, Jeff, and Sand, Gary, **Fighter Command**, Osceola, WI, Motorbooks, 1991, 176 p., illus., all color, hard bound.
9th AF	533	**Desert Campaign**, Printing and Stationery Services (British Army unit), 1943, 140 p.
9th AF	534	Marx, Milton, Paris, France, Desfosses-Neogravure, 1945, 26 p. color illus. Original action paintings.
9th AF	535	Bozung, Jack H. **The 9th Sees France and England**, Los Angeles, CA, AAF Publication Co., 1947, 40 p., illus.
9th AF	536	Rust, Kenn C., **The 9th Air Force in World War II**, Fallbrook, Ca, Aero Publishers, Inc., 1967, 245 p., illus., line drawings, dust cover has unit crest in color, hard bound.
9th AF	537	Rust, Kenn C., **Ninth Air Force Story**, Temple City, CA, Historical Aviation Album, 1982, 64 p., illus., line drawings, color on cover. Soft cover. Reprinted by Sunshine House, Terre Haute, IN, 1992
9th AF	538	Hamlin, John F., **Support and Strike**, London, Eng., GMS Enterprises, 1991128 p., illus, soft cover.
10th AF	539	Weaver, Herbert and Rapp, Marvin, 1944, 178 p., Reprinted by Sunflower University Press.
10th AF	540	Hq, AAF, **Highlights**, New York, 1945, 9 p. Reproduced from typed copy.
10th AF	541	Russell, W.W., **Forgotten Skies**, London, Eng., Hutchinson, 1945, 128 p., illus., hard bound.

10th AF	542	Rust, Kenn C., **Tenth Air Force Story**, Temple City, CA, Historical Aviation Album, 1980, 64 p., color on cover. Soft Cover. Reprinted by Sunshine House, Terre Haute, IN, 1992.
11th AF	543	Cloe, John H., **The Aleutian Warriors**, Missoula, MT, Pictorial Histories Publishing Co., Inc., 1992, 344 p., illus., soft cover.
12th AF	544	Hq, AAF, **The AAF In Northwest Africa,** Washington, DC, Govt Printing Office, 1945, 67 p., illus., cover in color.
12th AF	545	HQ, AAF, **The AAF In The Invasion of Southern France**, Washington, DC, Govt. Printing Office, 1945, 60 p., illus., cover in color.
12th AF	546	Bozung, Jack, **The Twelfth Over the Mediterranean**, Los Angeles, CA, AAF Publications Co., 40 p., illus.
12th AF	547	Engle, Richard A. and Larson, John W., HQ, Twelfth Air Force, Kaiserlautern, Ger., 1956, 58 p., illus.
12th AF	548	Rust, Kenn C. , **Twelfth Air Force Story**, Historical Aviation Album, Temple City, CA, 1975, 64 p., illus., cover in color. Soft cover. Reprinted by Sunshine House, Terre Haute, IN, 1992.
13th Bomb Cmd	549	Hq, XIII Bomber Command, 905th Eng. Co., 1944, 160 p. Reproduced from typed copy.
13th AF	550	Lippincott, Benjamin E., **From Fiji Through The Philippines With the Thirteenth Air Force**, San Angelo, TX, Newsfoto Publishing Co., 1948, 193 p., illus. with original art (some in full color) by Robert A. Laessig. Hard Bound cover portrays XIII crest in color.
13th AF	551	Bell, Dana and Rust, Kenn C., **Thirteenth Air Force Story**, Temple City, Ca, Historical Aviation Album, 1981, 64 p., illus., cover in color. Soft cover. Reprinted by Sunshine House, Terre Haute, IN, 1992.
14th AF	552	MCClure, Glenn E., **Fire and Fall Back**, San Antonio, TX, Barnes Press, 1975, 256 p., illus., sketches by Milton Caniff, color on dust cover, hard bound.
14th AF	553	Muth, Stephen and Rust, Kenn C., **Fourteenth Air Force Story**, Temple City, CA, Historical Aviation Album, 1977, 64 p., illus., cover in color. Soft cover. Reprinted by Sunshine House, Terre Haute, IN, 1992.
14th AF	554	Rosholt, Malcolm, **Days Of The Ching Pao**, Amherst, WI, Palmer Publications Inc., 1978, 192 p., illus., color on dust cover, hard bound.
14th AF	555	Johnson, Wayne G. and Van Cleve, Don, **Chennault's Flying Tigers: A Pictorial History of the AVG, China Air Task Force, 14th Air Force, 1941-1945**, Dallas, TX, 1983, 123 p., illus.
14th AF	556	**Chennault's Flying Tigers**, 1941-1945, two vol., Dallas, TX, Taylor Publishing Co., 1983, 125 p. each, illus., hardbound.
14th AF	557	Chennault, Max, **Up Sun**, 142 p., soft bound.
14th AF	558	Miller, **Tiger Tales**, 1991, 155 p., illus., softbound.

15th AF	559	**The Air Battle of Ploesti Written in the Skies Over Romania By the U.S. Fifteenth Air Force and the 205 Group (RAF) Between 5 April and 19 August 1944**, 941st Eng. Be., 1945, 108 p., illus.
15th AF	560	Bozung, Jack H., **The 15th Over Italy**, Los Angeles, CA, AAF Publications, 1947, 40 p., illus.
15th AF	561	Rust, Kenn C., **Fifteenth Air Force Story** , Temple City, CA, Historical Aviation Album,. 1976, 64 p., illus., line drawings, cover in color. Reprinted by Sunshine House, Terre Haute, IN 1992.
19th TAC	562	Hq, AF, **Air Ground Teamwork on the Western Front**, Washington, DC, Govt. Printing Office, 1945, 50 p., illus., cover in color.
19th TAC	563	Stars and Stripes, **Fly, Seek, and Destroy**, Paris, Fr., Desfosses-Neogravure, 1945, 32 p., illus.
20th AF	564	Hq, AAF, **Highlights**, New York, NY 1945, 9 p. Reproduced from typed copy.
20th AF	565	Bozung, Jack H., **The 20th Over Japan**, Los Angeles, CA AAF Publications, 1946, 40 p., illus.
20th AF	566	N. Finkelstein, **Memorial Album**, Los Angeles, Ca, Economy Typesetting Service, 1951, 134 p.
20th AF	567	USAF, **Resume: 20th Air Force Missions**, Washington, DC, 1969, 183 p., illus.
20th AF	568	Morrison, Wilbur H., **Point of No Return**, New York, NY, New York Times, 1979, 278 p., illus.
20th AF	569	Rust, Kenn C., **Twentieth Air Force Story**, Temple City, CA, Historical Aviation, 1979, 64 p., illus., cover in color. Soft bound. Reprinted by Sunshine House, Terre Haute, IN, 1992.
20th AF	570	Marshall, Chester W., **The Global Twentieth**, Vol I, Memphis, TN, Global Press, 1985, 400 p., illus., hard bound.
20th AF	571	Marshall, Chester W., **The Global Twentieth**, Vol II,
20th AF	572	Marshall, Chester W., Silverster, Lindsey, and Stallings, Scotty, **The Global Twentieth**, Vol. III, Memphis, TN, Global Press, 1989, 396 p., illus., hard bound.
29th TAC	573	US Army, **Mission Accomplished**, Paris, Fr., Desfosses-Neogravure, 1945, 31 p., illus.

U.S. NAVY UNITS
Navy Squadrons

VF-1	**574**	United States Navy, **High Hatters,** 1945, 71 p., illus.
VT-1	**575**	1945
VB-2	**576**	Buell, Harold L., **Dauntless Helldivers,** New York, NY, Orion Books, 1991, 348 p., illus., hard cover. Personal narrative.
VF-2	**577**	Morrissey, Thomas L., **Odyssey of Fighting Two,** 1945, 207 p., illus.
VT-4	**578**	Thomas, Gerald W., **A Cockpit View of World War II,** Las Cruces, NM, The Rio Grande Historical Collections, New Mexico State U., 1991, 249 p., illus., soft bound. Personal narrative.
VS-6	**579**	Dickinson, Clarence E., **The Flying Guns: Cockpit Record of a Naval Pilot From Pearl Harbor Through Midway,** New York, NY, Charles Scribners, 1942, 196 p., illus. Personal narrative. Reprinted by Zenger Publishing Co., Washington, D.C., in 1980.
VT -8	**580**	Mears, Frederick, **Carrier Combat,** Garden City, NY, Doubleday, Doran and Co., 1943, 156 p.
VT-8	**581**	Wolfert, Ira, **Torpedo 8: The Story of Swede Larson's Bomber Squadron,** Boston, MA, Houghton Mifflin, 1943, 127 p., hard bound.
VT-8	**582**	Gay, George H., **Sole Survivor,** Marietta, GA, Midway Publications, 1979, 320 p., illus., hard cover. Personal narrative.
VF-10	**583**	Johnston, Stanley, **The Grim Reapers,** New York, NY, E.P. Dutton & Co., Inc., 1943, 221 p., illus., hardbound.
VF-10	**584**	Mersky, Peter, **The Grim Reapers,** Yuma, AZ, Champlin Fighter Museum Press, 1986, 131 p., illus., soft cover.
VB-17	**585**	Olds, Robert, **Helldiver Squadron,** New York, NY, Dodd, Mead, 1944, 263 p., illus., hard bound. Reprinted by Zenger Publishing Co.,Washington, D.C. 1980.
VF-17 & VBF-17	**586**	**The Hellcat Squadrons,** 1945, 22 p., illus.
VF-17	**587**	Blackburn, Tom, **The Jolly Rogers,** New York, NY, Orion Books, 1990, 288 p., illus., original art on dust jacket, hard bound. Personal narrative.
VT-17	**588**	San Francisco, CA, James H. Barry Co., 1945, 67 p., illus.
VF-18	**589**	Forsyth, John F., **Hell Divers,** Osceola, WI, Motorbooks International, 1991, 160 p., illus., color on cover, softbound. Personal narrative.
VF-18	**590**	San Francisco, CA, 1944, 64 p., illus.
VF-19	**591**	Winters, Hugh T., **Skipper: Confessions of a Fighter Squadron Commander 1943-1944,** 158 p., illus., hard bound. Personal narrative.

VF-31	592	Winston, Robert A., **Fighting Squadron: A Veteran Squadron Leader's First-Hand Account of Carrier Combat with Task Force 58**, New York, NY, Holiday, 1946, 182 p., illus., hard bound. Reprinted by Naval Institute Press 1991. Personal narrative.
VPB-33	593	Mueller, A.J. **Black Cats with Wings of Gold**, Philadaelphia, PA, Smith-Edwards-Dunlap Co., 1992, 140 p., illus. hard bound
VPB-34	594	Hayes, Robert, **Bless 'em All**, Willow Creek Publications, Eden Prairie, MN, 1986, 88 p., illus. Personal narrative.
VF-46	595	Ziesing, Hibben, New York, NY, 1946, 43 p., illus.
VT-50	596	**Nine Out of Fifty**, 1945, 43 p., illus.
VT-51	597	Hyams, Joe, **Flight of the Avenger**, Orlando, FL, Harcourt Brace, Javonovich, 1991, 178 p., illuls., hard bound. Personal narrative.
VC-63	598	Anderson, Norman J., **Composite Squadron 63** Baton Rouge, LA, Army & Navy Publishing, 1946, 80 p., illus
VP-63	599	**Along The Way**, 1945, 76 p., illus., hard bound.
VC-77	600	Rice, J.L., **It Just So Happens**, 1945, 44 p., illus.
VP-81	601	**Black Cats**, 1945, 102 p., illus.
VF-85	602	Stratford, CT, 1945, 88 p., illus.
VF-89, VBF-89	603	**Pied Pipers**, 1946, 80 p., illus.
VPB-104	604	**Buccaneers, First Tour, Apr 43-Apr 44**, 37 p., illus.
VPB-104	605	**Third Tour, June 1945-October 1945**, Baltimore, MD, Schneidereith, 1945, 48 p., illus.
VPB-106	606	Hastings, Robert P., **Privateer in the Coconut Navy**, 1946, 105 p., illus.
VPB-109	607	Miller, Norman M., and Cave, Hugh B., **I Took the Sky Road,** New York, NY, Dodd, Mead, & Co..1945, 212 p., illus. Personal narrative of squadron CO.
VPB-121	608	Corwin, O.M., Jr., **Battle Diary** San Diego, CA, Frye Printing, 1945, 55 p., illus.
VB-148	609	Berkeley, CA, Lederer, 1944, 36 p., illus.
VPB-153	610	Guam, 64th Eng. Topo Bn., 1945, 20 p., illus.
VT-305	611	Kepchia, John B., **M.I.A. Over Rabaul, South Pacific**, Greensburgh, PA, The Palace Printer, 1986, 145 p., illus., soft cover. Personal narrative of radio gunner who was P.O.W.

CARRIER AIR GROUPS

CAG-2	**612**	Nelson, Ken, **Oriental Odyssey**, 1945, 75 p., illus.
CAG-6	**613**	Gerler, William R., 1945, 100 p., illus.
CAG-6	**614**	Stafford, Edward P., **The Big E**, New York, NY, Dell Publishing Co., 1962, 512 p., illus., pocket book.
CAG-9	**615**	**Second Pacific Cruise, March 1944-July 1945**, Allentown, PA, Sanders, 1945, 180 p., illus.
CAG-10	**616**	1945, 176 p., illus.
CAG-15	**617**	Hoyt, Edwin P., **McCampbell's Heroes**, New York, NY, Van Norstrand, 1983, 189 p., illus., hard bound.
CAG-16	**618**	Beyan, Joseph I. and Reed, Philip G., **Mission beyond Darkness**, New York, NY, Duell, Sloan and Pearce, 1945, 133 p., illus.
CAG-20	**619**	1949, 85 p., illus.
CAG-47	**620**	Chicago, IL, Smith, 1945, 40 p., illus.
CAG-81	**621**	**Prep Charlie**, New York, NY, 1945, 206 p., illus.
CAG-86	**622**	Camp, Robert Jr., 1946, 140 p., illus.

CAG-16 + OTHERS — HOYT, EDWIN P. THE BATTLE OF LEYTE GULF, 1972 346 PAGES, ILLUS.

A.G. 12, AG 23, TF-31,38,39 / TF-58 — CORTESI, LAWRENCE, OPERATION CARTWHEEL KENSINGTON PUB. 1982

AIRCRAFT CARRIERS

Belleau Wood
CVL-24
623 **Flight Quarters**, Alexander, John, Los Angeles, CA, Cole, Holmquist Press, 1946, 191 p., hardbound, illus. Reprinted by CVL-24 Assn. in 1991.

Bennington
CV-20
624 1945, 66 p., illus.

Bunker Hill
CV-17
625 Chicago, 1944, 271 p., illus.

Cabot
CVL-28
626 Hudson, J., 1986, 179 p., illus., hard bound.

Chenango
CVE-28
627 Los Angeles, CA, Kater, 1945, 64 p., illus.

Enterprise
CV-6
628 Burns, Eugene, **Then There Was One: The USS Enterprise and the First Year of War,** New York, NY, Harcourt Brace, 1944 179 p., illus. Hardbound.

Essex
CV-9
629 Markey, Morris, **Well Done** New York, NY, D. Appleton-Century Co., 1945, 223 p., illus.

Essex
CV-9
630 **Saga of the Essex**, Baton Rouge, LA, Army & Navy Publishing, 1946, 167 p., illus.

Franklin
CV-13
631 **Big Ben**, Atlanta, GA, Love, 1946, 68 p., illus.

Gambier Bay
CVE-73
632 Hoyt, Edwin P., **The Men of the Gambier Bay**, Middlebury, VT, Paul S. Erickson Publisher, 1979, 254 p., illus.

Hancock
CV-19
633 Hines, E.G., **The Fighting Hannah**, Nashville, TN, 1945, 142 p., illus.,

Hornet
CV-12
634 **First War Cruise, 1943-1945,** lithographed on board, 1945, 48 p., illus.

Intrepid
CV-11
635 Los Angeles, CA, Metropolitan Engraving, 1946, 168 p., illus.

Lexington
CV-2
636 Johnston, Stanley, **Queen of the FlatTops**, New York, NY, E.P. Dutton & Co., Inc., 1942, Reprinted by Bantam Books, 1979, 234 p., original sketches., pocket book.

Lexington
CV-2 and CV-16
637 Ewing, Steve, **The Lady Lex and the Blue Ghost**, 1989, 44 p., pictorial history, hard bound.

Lexington
CV-16
638 **Tarawa to Tokyo**, 1946, 82 p., illus.

Lexington
CV-16
639 Reese, Lee F., **Men of the Blue Ghost**, San Diego, CA, 1947. Revised and enlarged edition published 1980, 923 p., illus.

Lexington
CV-16
640 Steichen, Edward, **The Blue Ghost: A Photographic Log and Personal Narrative**, New York, NY, Harcourt Brace, 1947, 151 p., illus.

Lunga Point
CVE-94
641 1945, 240 p., illus.

Makassar Strait
CVE-91
642 **The Mighty Mak**, Seattle, WA, 1946, 37 p., illus.

Randolph
CV-15
643 **The Gangway**, 1946, 80 p., illus.

Savo Island
CVE-78
644 Benton, Brantford B., **Battle Baby: A Pictorial History**, Baton Rouge, LA, Army & Navy Publishing Co., 1946, 132 p., illus.

Suwanee CVE-27	**645**	Green, Peyton, **Five Thousand Miles Towards Tokyo**, Norman, OK, University of Oklahoma Press, 1945, 173 p., illus.
Suwanee CVE-27	**646**	Baton Rouge, LA, Army & Navy Publishing, 1946, 87 p., illus.
Takanis Bay CVE-89	**647**	1946., 60 p., illus.
Ticonderoga CV-14	**648**	**War Log**, Baton Rouge, LA, Army & Navy Publishing Co.,1945, 153 p., illus.
Wasp CV-18	**649**	Boston, MA, Crosby, 1946, 106 p., illus.
Yorktown CV-10	**650**	**Into The Wind**, 1945, 160 p., illus.
Yorktown CV-5	**651**	Cressman, **The Gallant Ship**, 1989, 184 p., illus.
Yorktown CV-5 & CV-10	**652**	Kitchen, Ruben P., Jr., **Pacific Carrier**, New York, NY, Kensington Publishing Corp., 1980, 319 p., pocket book.
Yorktown CV-10	**653**	Reynolds, Clark, **The Fighting Lady**, 1989, 355 p. illus.

NAVY AIR WINGS

Flt Air Wg 4   **654**   Scrivner, Charles L., **The Empire Express**, Temple City, CA, Historical Aviation Album, 1976, 56 p., illus., aircraft profiles, color on cover.

Flt Air Wg 4   **655**   See Eleventh Air Force reference.

Pat Wg 4   **656**   Thorburn, Don and Lois, **No Tumult, No Shouting**, New York, NY, Henry Holt & Co., 1945, 148 p., illus. hard bound.

Pat Wg 10   **657**   Messimer, Dwight R., **In The Hands of Fate**, Annapolis, MD, Naval Institute Press, 1985, 350 p., illus., original art on dust jacket, hard bound.

US MARINE CORPS UNITS

VMO-6	658	Parker, Gary W. and Batha, Frank M., Washington D.C., Marine Corps Historical Center, 1982, 73 p., illus., soft cover. History of unit from 1920 through Vietnam.
VMF-115	659	Chapin, John C., Washington, DC, Marine Corps Historical Center, 1982, 73 p., illus., soft cover. History of unit in WW II and post war.
VMF-121	660	Simmons, Walter, **Joe Foss, Flying Marine**, New York, NY, E.P. Dutton & Co., 1943, 160 p., illus. hard bound. Biography of author.
VMF-122	661	Reinburg, J. Hunter, **Combat Aerial Escapades**, New York, NY, Carlton Press, 1966, 165 p., hard bound. Personal narrative of pilot who served with VMF-121, 122, 225. Reprinted in 1990 by author.
VMF-211	662	Heinl, R.D., Jr., **The Defense of Wake**, USMC, 1947
VMF-211	663	Cohen, **Enemy on the Island-Issue in Doubt: The Capture of Wake Island, December 1941**, 116 p., illus.
VMF-211	664	Schultz, Duane, **Wake Island**, New York, NY, St. Martins Press, 1978, 247 p., illus. hard bound.
VMF-214	665	Boyington, Gregory, **Baa Baa Black Sheep**, New York, NY, G.P. Putman's Sons, 1958, 384 p., hard bound. Republished by TAB, and in pocket book form by Bantam.
VMF-214	666	Walton, Frank L., **Once They Were Eagles**, Lexington, KY, University Press of Kentucky, 1986, 248 p., illus. hard bound.
VMF-222	667	Foster, John M., **Hell in the Heavens**, New York, NY, G.P. Putman's Sons/ Ace Books, 1961, 254 p., pocket bok. Personal narrative. Reprinted by Zenger Publishing Co. , Washington, D.C., 1981.
VMF 223	668	Jones, Brett A., Washington, D.C., Marine Corps Historical Center, 1978, 39 p., illus., soft cover. History of unit in WW II, Vietnam and post-war.
VMF-225	669	See VMF-122 reference.
VMF-232	670	Sambito, William J., Washington, D.C., Marine Corps Historical Center, 1978, 67 p., illus., soft cover. History of unit from 1925 through Vietnam.
VMTB-232	671	Hynes, Samuel, **Flights of Passage**, Annapolis, MD, Frederic C. Beil, Naval Institute Press, 1988, 270 p., hard bound. Personal narrative.
VMF-311	672	Sambito, William J., Washington, D.C., Marine Corps Historical Center, 1978, 67 p., illus., soft cover. History of from WW II, Vietnam and post-war.
VMF-312	673	Sambito, William J., Washington, D.C., Marine Corps Historical Center, 1978, 25 p., illus., soft bound. History of unit in WW II, Korea, Vietnam.
VMF-321	674	Mersky, Peter B., Washington, D.C., Marine Corps Historical Center, 1991, 47 p., illus., soft cover. History of unit from WW II to postwar.

VMF-323	**675**	Pitzel, Gerald R., Washington, D.C., Marine Corps Historical Center, 1987, 61 p., illus., soft cover. History of unit 1943-1986, including combat in WW II, Korea and Vietnam.
VMF(N)-533 & VMF(N)-542	**676**	Porter, Robert B. and Hammel, Eric, **Ace**, Pacifica, CA 1985, 279 p., illus., hard bound. Reprinted by Presidio Press, 1988, 300 p., illus. Personal narrative.
VMB-611	**677**	Perry, Raymond, **The Bombers of Magzam**, 1945, 110 p., illus.
VMB-612	**678**	Honeycutt, Thomas D., **Cram's Rams**, 1989, 468 p., illus.

EAGLE SQUADRONS

679 Kennerly, Byron, **The Eagles Roar**, New York, NY, Harper & Bros., 1942, 271 p. ,illus., hardbound. Personal narrative of 71 Squadron pilot. Reprinted by Zenger Publishing Co., 1981.

680 Childers, James Saxon, **War Eagles**, New York, NY, D. Appleton-Century Co., 1943, 350 p., illus., hard bound.

681 Haugland, Vern, **The Eagle Squadrons**, New York, NY, Ziff-Davis, 1979, 206 p., illus., hardbound.

682 Haugland, Vern, **The Eagle's War: The Saga of the Eagle Squadron Pilots, 1940-1945**, New York, NY, Jason Aronson, 1982, 234 p., illus. Also covers service with 4th Fighter Group.

AMERICAN VOLUNTEER GROUP

683 Whelan, Russell, **The Flying Tigers**, New York, NY, The Viking Press, 1942, 224 p., illus., hard bound.

684 Bond, Charles R. and Anderson, Terry H., **A Flying Tiger's Diary**, College Station, TX, Texas A&M University Press, 1984, 248 p., illus., hardbound. Personal narrative.

685 Smith, R. T., **Tale of a Tiger**, Van Nuys, CA, Tiger Originals, 1990, 384 p., illus., hardbound. Personal narrative.

686 Ford, Dan, **Flying Tigers: Claire Chennault and the American Volunteer Group**, Washington D.C., Smithsonian Institute Press, 1991, 650 p., illus. hardbound.

TOLAND, JOHN "THE FLYING TIGERS" DELL 1963

SCHULTZ, DUANE "THE MAVERICK WAR: CHENNAULT AND THE FLYING TIGERS" 1987 ST MARTINS PRESS

OTHER DEFINITIVE MILITARY/AVIATION HISTORIES
By
PHALANX PUBLISHING CO., LTD.:

The Pineapple Air Force: Pearl Harbor to Tokyo
by John Lambert $44.95

Republic P-47 Thunderbolt, The Final Chapter: Latin American Air Forces Service
by Dan Hagedorn $14.95

Eagles of Duxford: The 78th Fighter Group in World War II
by Garry Fry $29.95

Kearby's Thunderbolts: The 348th Fighter Group in World War II
by John Stanaway $24.95

Wildcats Over Casablanca
by John Lambert $11.95

B-25 Mitchell: The Magnificent Medium
by Norm Avery $29.95

FORTHCOMING TITLES

Air To Air
Tales of aerial combat by Henry Sakaida

Messerschmitt Roulette
The Desert War from a Hurricane Recce Pilot of No 451 Squadron RAAF by Wing Commander
Geoffrey Morley-Mower, DFC, RAF (ret.)

The 1st Fighter Group in World War II
The MTO war of the this legendary P-38 unit by one of its pilots, John D. Mullins

The Sundowners
World War II history of VF-11 on two combat tours, by Barrett Tillman

Fantail Fighters
Battleship and cruiser floatplanes in World War II, by Jerry Scutts

The Yoxford Boys
The 357th Fighter Group in Europe, by Merle Olmsted.   SEE PG 23

Marine Mitchells
U.S. Marine Corps opertions with PBJ aircraft in the Pacific, by Jerry Scutts